...e Holy Spirit offer us either light or heat. ...atest offering is admirable in its zeal for the subject ...cts a zeal according to knowledge. Keener has an irenic ...pirit, a fine mind, and a heart for the Lord, and this shows on every page of the book. Those wishing to walk successfully through the minefield of questions (without blowing up) that both the Bible and contemporary experience raise will find this a welcome guide. I heartily commend it."

Ben Witherington, III, professor of New Testament interpretation
Asbury Theological Seminary, Kentucky

3 Crucial
Questions
about the
Holy Spirit

W. B. Richardson

e and Richard J. Jones, Jr., editors

al Questions about Jesus
Murray J. Harris
3 Crucial Questions about the Bible
Grant R. Osborne
3 Crucial Questions about the Holy Spirit
Craig S. Keener
3 Crucial Questions about Spiritual Warfare (forthcoming)
Clinton E. Arnold
3 Crucial Questions about the Old Testament (forthcoming)
Tremper Longman III
3 Crucial Questions about Women (forthcoming)
Linda L. Belleville
3 Crucial Questions about Black Theology (forthcoming)
Bruce J. Fields
3 Crucial Questions about the Last Days (forthcoming)
Daniel J. Lewis
3 Crucial Questions about the Trinity (forthcoming)
Millard J. Erickson
3 Crucial Questions about Salvation (forthcoming)
Richard J. Jones, Jr.
3 Crucial Questions about Moral Reasoning (forthcoming)
Kevin J. Vanhoozer
3 Crucial Questions about Racial Reconciliation (forthcoming)
Raleigh B. Washington

Other Books by Craig S. Keener

And Marries Another: Divorce and Remarriage in the Teaching of the New Testament

Paul, Women, and Wives: Marriage and Women's Ministry in the Letters of Paul

The IVP Bible Background Commentary: New Testament

Black Man's Religion: Can Christianity Be Afrocentric (with Glenn Usry)

The Spirit in the Gospels and Acts

3 Crucial
Questions
about the
Holy Spirit

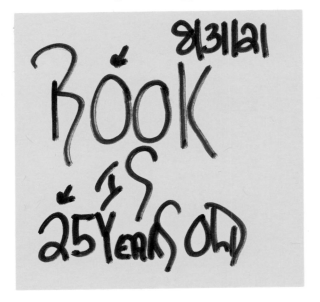

Baker Books

A Division of Baker Book House Co
Grand Rapids, Michigan 49516

Published by Baker Books
a division of Baker Book House Company
P.O. Box 6287, Grand Rapids, MI 49516–6287

Printed in the United States of America

ISBN 0–8010–5592-X
Cataloging information is on file at the Library of Congress, Washington, D.C.

To the memory of Pentecostal church planters
Everett and Esther Cook,
two of my earliest mentors in ministry

Contents

Editors' Preface   9
Author's Preface   11
Acknowledgments   15

1. **What Is the "Baptism in the Holy Spirit"?**   17
2. **How Important Are Spiritual Gifts Today?**   79
3. **How Can We Recognize the Spirit?**   131

Conclusion   181
Appendix: What Can Bible Stories Teach Us?   185
Notes   191
Selected Bibliography   201
Scripture Index   205

Editors' Preface

The books in the 3 Crucial Questions series are the published form of the 3 Crucial Questions Seminars, which are sponsored by Bridge Ministries of Detroit, Michigan. The seminars and books are designed to greatly enhance your Christian walk. The following comments will help you appreciate the unique features of the book series.

The 3 Crucial Questions series is based on two fundamental observations. First, there are crucial questions related to the Christian faith for which imperfect Christians seem to have no final answers. Christians living in eternal glory may know fully even as they are known by God, but now we know only in part (1 Cor. 13:12). Therefore, we must ever return to such questions with the prayer that God the Holy Spirit will continue to lead us nearer to "the truth, the whole truth, and nothing but the truth." While recognizing their own frailty, the authors contributing to this series pray that they are thus led.

Second, each Christian generation partly affirms its solidarity with the Christian past by reaffirming "the faith which was once delivered unto the saints" (Jude 3 KJV). Such an affirmation is usually attempted by religious scholars who are notorious for talking only to themselves or by nonexperts whose grasp of the faith lacks depth of insight. Both situations are unfortunate, but we feel that our team of contributing authors is well prepared to avoid them. Each author is a competent Christian scholar able to share tremendous learning in down-to-earth language both laity and experts can appreciate. In a word, you have in hand a book that is part of a rare series, one that is neither pedantic nor pediatric.

The topics addressed in the series have been chosen for their timelessness, interest level, and importance to Christians everywhere. And the contributing authors are committed to discussing them in a manner that promotes Christian unity. Thus, they discuss not only areas of disagreement among Christians but significant areas of agreement as well. Seeking peace and pursuing it as the Bible commands (1 Peter 3:11), they stress common ground on which Christians with different views may meet for wholesome dialogue and reconciliation.

The books in the series consist not merely of printed words; they consist of words to live by. Their pages are filled not only with good information but with sound instruction in successful Christian living. For study is truly Christian only when, in addition to helping us understand our faith, it helps us to live our faith. We pray therefore that you will allow God to use the 3 Crucial Questions series to augment your growth in the grace and knowledge of our Lord and Savior Jesus Christ.

Grant R. Osborne
Richard J. Jones, Jr.

Author's Preface

This book differs from some other works in this series (for instance, Murray Harris's arguments for Christ's deity and bodily resurrection) in that this book addresses an issue on which there is no absolute consensus among Christians. When we discuss the activity of the Spirit, as when we discuss the events of the end time, we must do so graciously, recognizing that not all Christians, not even all evangelicals, speak with one mind.[1]

This caution is all the more important for a topic like this one, where one's experience (or nonexperience) affects one's perceptions of what the early church's experience may have been. So I admit at the outset some of my Christian experience: I have been miraculously healed, experienced supernatural gifts like prophecy, and had deep experiences in the Spirit during prayer that make it virtually impossible for me even to consider the position that such experiences do not belong to today's church. I view these experiences as an asset in writing a book on the Holy Spirit, but others may think them a liability that will bias my findings. Yet I hope that in the unity of Christ's Spirit, we will continue to treat one another with respect and Christian love. The points of agreement all Christians share on matters of the Spirit far outnumber our points of disagreement. I have ministered alongside brothers and sisters who believe that supernatural gifts have ceased and also with charismatics of the sort whose doctrine I would consider extreme. I value my friends and colleagues who teach at traditionally cessationist schools (schools teaching that supernatural gifts have ceased) and those who teach at traditional Pentecostal schools. Our differences on these points do not divide us on the central issue of Christ's lordship and our mission to disciple the nations for him.

When I was invited to contribute to this series, I had not planned to write a book of this nature on the Spirit. The topic I suggested was racial reconciliation, with the Spirit as my second choice. But the Spirit was the topic my editors preferred, probably because it relates to my dissertation area and because I have simultaneously been writing a scholarly work on the subject for Hendrickson Publishers. That my editors granted me much latitude in addressing the topic, knowing that I am charismatic in my personal prayer experience, testifies to the degree of cooperation that is emerging on the issue of the Spirit in evangelicalism today. They only wanted to make sure that I was a "sound" charismatic "like Gordon Fee." Besides Gordon Fee, a number of other mainstream evangelical scholars who are openly charismatic include Peter Davids, Michael Green, Wayne Grudem, and Ben Witherington, as well, I am told, as some widely read evangelical writers like Martin Lloyd-Jones. Not all charismatics, of course, share all the same views about the Spirit and spiritual gifts.

Although this book demands that I listen with an open heart to the views of the whole church, my priority as a biblical scholar is to listen first and foremost to the biblical text. My own background (charismatic, but also a Baptist minister who wrote this book while teaching in an African Methodist Episcopal Zion seminary) undoubtedly affects the way I approach this subject, and I expect writers from other backgrounds to challenge me as we work together seeking to discover more clearly what Scripture teaches. Yet I genuinely want to hear the Spirit-inspired message of the prophets and apostles of Scripture, rather than my own traditions.

I have endeavored to be sensitive to the wide audience a book like this one will obtain and to be alert to how various statements might be read, seeking to incorporate what I believe are valid insights from both charismatic and noncharismatic positions. I doubt that every reader will agree on every point, but I believe that much of the church, both charismatic and noncharismatic, is moving beyond many of the disputes that have divided us in the past. Most Christians today recognize both that spiritual gifts are biblical and that Christ, not His gifts, must represent the *ultimate* object of our devotion. As a charismatic Baptist minister and professor, I earnestly believe that all of us—from the most traditional Pentecostals to the staunchest cessationists—need a deeper sensitivity to the Holy Spirit's empowerment in our lives. Readers from various backgrounds may disagree on some aspects of my attempt to pull together what I believe are the best insights of different positions, but whether readers agree with such attempts in detail is ultimately of minimal importance. The basic thrust is far more essential: the early Christians were dependent on God's Spirit from start to finish, and we must be too.

Each revival movement in history has experienced a fresh outpouring of God's Spirit, generally accompanied by some phenomena (admittedly sometimes excessive) that threatened the comfortable theological systems of the ecclesiastical status quo. Yet the strength of the flesh, or proud human intellect that seeks to control God's power by reducing it to terms we can explain, can pretend to be sufficient for God's work only when the kingdom of Satan appears to be dormant. Now is not such a time. Those of us involved in various forms of frontline evangelism recognize that our nation now has little time; we now stand in desperate need of revival. Will we dare to submit our lives to the giver of the Spirit, regardless of what price the Spirit may call us to pay to reach our contemporaries for Christ? On the answer to that question hangs the fate of our generation.

Acknowledgments

I wish to thank some dear brothers and sisters, both charismatic and noncharismatic, who allowed me to bounce ideas off them while I tried to nuance my words just right. I must especially mention Melesse and Tadesse Woldetsadik, two charismatic brothers from Ethiopia who led hundreds of people to Christ while living in refugee camps, and whose hospitality in Christ has often refreshed me. I also thank Sharon Saunders, a Baptist missionary and dear friend whose sending agency, Africa Inland Mission, graciously forwarded my heavy packages to her; her vibrant prayer life and love for our Lord have often provoked me to deeper zeal for God. Jackie Reeves, a charismatic African Methodist Episcopal minister in New Jersey, has been like a mother in the Lord to me, and her prayers and wisdom have also proved invaluable.

I thank my series editors, Richard Jones and Grant Osborne, and Jim Weaver of Baker Book House for welcoming my contribution to the series and Wells Turner for copyediting the work. Richard recommended most of the works included in this book's brief bibliography. I must also thank Bridge Ministries of Detroit and Trinity Evangelical Divinity School for sponsoring the seminar at Circle Urban Ministries in Chicago in spring of 1996, which provided the basis for this book. Thanks is also due Chinese United Methodist Church in New York for allowing me to present most of this material during their retreat on the Holy Spirit in August 1995.

Everett and Esther Cook, to whom this book is dedicated, spent much of the century pioneering Pentecostal churches in the western United States. Afterward, they opened a street mission with their retirement income and mentored the college students who worked with them at the mission, treating us like their own children. Although they had not attended college and I was initially too impressed with my growing knowledge of biblical languages and culture to appreciate them as I should have, I ultimately learned from their lives of humble faithfulness what no book could have taught me.

What Is the "Baptism in the Holy Spirit"?

Consider the following illustration from a recent magazine article:

> Imagine visiting a town at night that appears to have no lights, no televisions—not even alarm clocks. And then imagine learning that the town's power supply is virtually infinite, but that no one in the town had thought to turn any of their electrical appliances on. Wouldn't that town seem like a silly place to you? Yet the Church is all too often like that town. God has given us the power of His Spirit to fulfill His mission in the world, yet few Christians have even begun to depend on His power.[1]

The Bible has more to say about the baptism in the Holy Spirit than what Christians today generally debate about. Thus, in the midst of current debates about *when* and *how* one is baptized in the Spirit, we often lose sight of *why* the Lord baptizes his followers in the Spirit. In this chapter we will survey the controversial "when" and "how" issues, but we will also include the more crucial "why" issue. We emphasize the "why" issue partly because Christians share more common ground on the Spirit than we often realize. All of us agree that all Christians have the Spirit by virtue of being born again. We also agree that we all should be filled with the Spirit in daily practice. Because we can all use a deeper daily empowerment of God's Spirit, we should all understand how deeply we need the Spirit for our service to God in this world and for living the Christian life.

So why do Christians debate so heatedly about issues like the baptism in the Spirit? In part it may be because we are speaking past each other. Most believers who insist that Spirit baptism occurs at conversion do not deny that God may fill believers with his Spirit in other ways after conversion. Conversely, most believers who insist that Spirit baptism generally occurs after conversion nevertheless agree that all believers receive the Spirit in the most important way at conversion. In other words, some of the most significant areas of disagreement today may be merely semantic. For example, some noncharismatics have reproved charismatics for using terms like "revelation" and "inspiration" for something other than Scripture, yet agree that God's Spirit can lead our daily lives, which is what most charismatics mean by the terms.

Often terms rather than concepts divide us, and often we do not even use the terms the way our own Bible translations do. Thus, as in the example above, we all agree that the Bible is the standard for evaluating claims that the Spirit is leading us; the Bible is the ultimate written "revelation." Yet whereas some limit the term "revelation" to the Bible alone, the biblical term translated "revelation" is not limited to Scripture. It can refer to a Damascus Road–type encounter with Christ (Gal. 1:12, 16) or to information revealed in prophecy (1 Cor. 14:26, 30; compare perhaps Gal. 2:2 with Acts 11:28–30). Likewise, many Christians apply the term "sanctification" to the biblical concept of maturing in Christ. But while maturing in Christ is a biblical notion, the New Testament almost never uses the term "sanctification" to describe that idea. If you scan New Testament references to "sanctification," you will discover that most texts refer to being set apart for God at conversion. However, other texts do indicate that we should learn to live like what God called us to be at our conversion.

We often assume particular working definitions of terms that are not shared by everyone else. By adopting some fairly neutral terms like "conversion" and "being filled with the Spirit" we could deal with the main issues with much less conflict. Consequently, when I teach publicly, I often prefer to bypass the semantic issue and emphasize the practical matter of seeking God's power to do his work. After all, the Bible *does* forbid us to argue over semantics (2 Tim. 2:14). This practical solution does not suggest, however, that it does not matter how the Bible uses phrases like "baptism in the Holy Spirit." Can different interpretations of that expression possibly be semantic differences too? After briefly considering that issue, we will explore the more central matter of what the Bible teaches about the Spirit's empowerment, including some insights that are not commonly discussed. Later in the chapter we will return briefly to the secondary question of whether baptism in the Spirit occurs during or after conversion.

Introducing the Timing Question

The controversy about when baptism in the Holy Spirit occurs in the believer's life has been around for some time and shows no signs of abating. Wesley and many of his followers became convinced that the Bible taught a second work of grace in the believer's life after conversion, in which the Spirit brought a believer to a higher level of inward purity.[2] Pursuit of this deeper experience of holiness became a common feature in North

American revivals of the mid- to late-nineteenth century. Finney, Moody, Torrey, and others viewed baptism in the Holy Spirit as an empowerment for service that was subsequent to conversion. The first Pentecostals thought that they had found a third experience in the Spirit (subsequent to both conversion and this second experience of "sanctification"), although other Pentecostals (today probably the majority) concluded that their experience was a second and final one, the baptism in the Holy Spirit. While no one should fault another Christian for seeking God's holiness more passionately, not everyone agrees that the expression "baptism in the Holy Spirit" applies to such a postconversion experience of God's Spirit. Many believe it applies only to conversion itself.

Thus most evangelical Christians today think of baptism in the Spirit in one of two ways: either Christians receiving the Spirit at conversion (the typical Reformed position) or Christians receiving a special empowerment after conversion (the usual Holiness and Pentecostal position). Those who emphasize the Bible's theological statements (such as Paul's comments) rather than narrative examples (such as stories in Acts) usually identify Spirit baptism with conversion to faith in Christ. Those who emphasize Acts over against Paul usually believe that Spirit baptism can occur after conversion.

Each tradition builds its case from some Bible texts, and it is possible that both traditions may be correctly interpreting their favored texts. I suspect (and will argue later in the chapter) that both groups of interpreters are in fact largely right. It appears that the New Testament teaches *both* views—for the simple reason that different texts employ the phrase "baptism in the Holy Spirit" in different ways. In other words, since most Christians agree that we receive the Spirit at conversion but can be filled afresh with the Spirit on later occasions, the biggest conflict on this issue today may be semantic. Someone might be tempted to think that such an approach is too convenient to be correct, but I believe and will argue below that this is the fairest way to read the biblical texts on their own terms.

That the phrase "baptism in the Spirit" could emphasize a different aspect of the Spirit's work in different biblical passages is not hard to understand once we recognize that these different emphases are all part of the work of the same Spirit. In view of the background we will look at below, it is likely that John the Baptist thought the Spirit's work involved a number of aspects, and that he was not focusing on one to the exclusion of others. Thus, when he promised that Jesus would baptize in the Holy Spirit, John probably used "baptism in the Spirit" to signify the *whole* work of the Spirit—including salvation and any subsequent empowerments. Similarly, whenever New Testament writers explain about believers receiving the Spirit, they invariably speak of the Spirit coming at the time of conversion (for example, Gal. 3:2; Acts 2:38). Christ's work is complete (Col. 2:6–23) and we cannot add to what God has provided for us in conversion (Rom. 5:5; Gal. 3:2–5).

Yet full access to God's transforming power at conversion need not imply that each of us has appropriated all that power in our daily lives. I suspect most of us will admit that in practice we may later yield more of our lives to the direction of God's Spirit. In narratives in the Book of Acts, examples indicate that believers embraced some aspects of the Spirit in an experience after their conversion (2:4; 8:15–16; 9:17; 19:4–6, treated below). Meanwhile, some other passages rarely cited by either side in the debate show us that the work of the Spirit not only means more than conversion but also more than any single subsequent experience. Acts indicates that believers may receive empowerments subsequent to their "second experience" (4:8, 31; 13:9). Paul likewise speaks of living a Spirit-filled life (Eph. 5:18), walking by the same Spirit one has already received (Gal. 5:16–23).

These passages suggest that the whole sphere of the Spirit's work becomes available at conversion, but believers may experience some aspects of the Spirit's work only subsequent to conversion. Once we lay the traditional semantic debates aside, this New Testament picture should make good sense to us in our own lives. One may compare other teachings in the New Testament about regularly appropriating Christ's finished work. For example, Paul teaches that believers become dead to sin at conversion; yet few of us dispute that we must learn to appropriate that reality in our daily lives. (Most Christians I know have sinned since their conversion.) Those interpreters who emphasize our completeness in Christ and the sufficiency of spiritual resources provided us in salvation are correct: when the Spirit enters our lives, God makes us new and gives us complete access to the Spirit's resources. At the same time, it is also biblical to emphasize that we need to draw on that empowerment in practice and that all Christians, no matter how full of God's Spirit, can grow to seek God more deeply.

We will address the "chronology" of Spirit baptism further below. But while this chronology is a topic of much debate among evangelicals today, it was not the primary feature of the baptism in the Spirit that the first Christians discussed. The New Testament in fact stresses features of Spirit baptism that are far more crucial to our daily Christian lives and yet are rarely discussed today. While much of the contemporary church has divided over whether baptism in the Spirit occurs at or after conversion, we have often neglected the sense of exactly what this baptism in the Spirit means for our daily lives in Christ. Whichever view we may take concerning the chronology of Spirit baptism (some readers may, with us, opt for both), all believers need to know what the Spirit means in practical terms for our relationship with Christ. In this chapter we trace some of the most important teachings about the baptism in the Holy Spirit in the New Testament. Only after we have done so will we return to the more controversial question of chronology.

Before we survey New Testament teachings about baptism in the Holy Spirit, we must get some background on the way Jesus' contemporaries thought about God's Spirit. Because they emphasized certain elements of what the Old Testament said about the Spirit, the first Christians could take for granted some ideas about the Spirit without explaining them. Once we understand some ideas that the New Testament writers took for granted, we will be ready to delve into New Testament perspectives on the baptism in the Spirit.[3]

What Did the Phrase "Baptism in the Holy Spirit" Mean to First-Century Hearers?

The phrase "baptism in the Holy Spirit" focuses on two primary elements: "baptize" and "Holy Spirit." "Baptize" is the easier of the two to summarize: Jewish people baptized Gentiles who wished to convert to Judaism by having them immerse themselves in water. The image of baptism thus connoted two ideas to ancient Jewish hearers: conversion and immersion. Those who identify Spirit baptism with conversion may support their case from the first image; those who identify it with a second work in which the Spirit overwhelms the believer (immersed in the Spirit) may appeal to the latter.

The second element of the phrase is the "Holy Spirit," which Jesus' Jewish contemporaries saw as God's way to purify his people or empower them to prophesy. The former image may support the idea that baptism in the Spirit occurs at conversion; the latter, that it reflects a subsequent experience of empowerment. Hence, the imagery by itself is not precise enough to solve the chronology question above.

The Bible tells us that the prophets of ancient Israel experienced the Spirit (1 Peter 1:10–11; 2 Peter 1:21; 1 Sam. 19:20–23; Ezek. 3:12); many of them must have wished that all their people would experience the Spirit more fully (Num.

11:29). By the seventh century B.C., Isaiah began to announce that God was going to make his Spirit more widely available. After judging his people, God would save and restore them, and pour out his Spirit on them like water on dry ground (Isa. 44:3; compare 42:1; 59:21). During the exile in Babylonia, the prophet Ezekiel made the same announcement: God would wash his people with the pure water of his Spirit (Ezek. 36:26–27), revive them by his Spirit (37:14), and pour out his Spirit on them (39:29). The prophet Joel announced that God would pour out his Spirit on his people—again using the image of the Spirit as water—and they would prophesy like the prophets of old (Joel 2:28–29).

But a few centuries before Jesus, many Jewish people decided that this full restoration of the Spirit and prophets belonged entirely to the distant future. They came to believe that prophets had ceased in their own time (although they allowed that prophecy occasionally continued) and that the Spirit was usually no longer available to individuals. A few groups, like the Essenes who wrote the Dead Sea Scrolls, believed that the Spirit remained active among them; but most Jews believed that the Spirit had been quenched in the present era. They longed for the future era when God would restore his people and pour out his Spirit.

Although all Jewish people were familiar with some Old Testament teachings on the Spirit, different Jewish groups emphasized different aspects of the Spirit. The two primary emphases were the Spirit of purification and the Spirit of prophecy. Some interpreters, especially the Essenes, noted that God would purify his people from sin as Ezekiel had prophesied (Ezek. 36:26–27; see also 18:31; 37:14). Nearly all Jews (including, to a lesser extent, the Essenes) associated the Spirit with prophecy, an even more common emphasis in the Old Testament (Num. 11:25–29; 2 Sam. 23:2; 2 Chron. 15:1–7; 18:23; Micah 3:8). Some New Testament teachings on the Holy Spirit—such as continual moral empowerment or God's presence within the individual believer—

rarely if ever occurred to these Jewish thinkers. But Jewish read-ers of the New Testament would have readily recognized early Christian emphases on the Spirit of purification (being "born of water and the Spirit") and prophecy (the Spirit enabling Chris-tians to prophesy or engage in other forms of inspired speech).

Many New Testament texts assume that readers understand the association of the Spirit with prophecy (Matt. 22:43; Luke 1:17; 2:27; 4:18; Acts 11:28; 21:4; 1 Cor. 7:40; 12:3; 1 Thess. 5:19; 1 Tim. 4:1; 1 Peter 1:11; 1 John 4:1–6; Rev. 1:10; 2:7; 3:6; 4:2; 14:13; 17:3; 19:10; 21:10; 22:17; compare 2 Thess. 2:2), including empowerment to speak for God in evangelism (Matt. 10:20; Acts 1:8; 6:10; 8:29; 10:19; 11:12; 16:7; 2 Cor. 3:3–8; Eph. 6:17), revelation of the true understanding of the gospel (1 Cor. 2:10–14; Eph. 1:17; 3:5), and apostolic miracles (Rom. 15:19; perhaps 1 Cor. 2:4). Other texts assume that we understand the import of the Spirit in giving life and in trans-formation (John 3:5–8; 1 Cor. 6:11; Gal. 4:29; 5:17–18; 6:8; Jude 19). These two streams of tradition represent the basic ideas about the Spirit over which many modern Christians have divided: the Spirit's role in conversion and the Spirit's role in empowering believers for inspired speech (tongues, prophecy, witness, etc.). Before returning to this question, we must exam-ine some of the New Testament's own essential emphases con-cerning baptism in the Holy Spirit.

"He Will Baptize in the Holy Spirit and Fire" (Matt. 3:11)

In contrast to Mark's abbreviated introduction, Matthew and Luke describe in greater detail John the Baptist's wilderness proclamation about the Spirit. To catch the full implications of his prophecy about the Spirit, we will first survey the more detailed form of John's sermon recorded in Matthew.

Keep in mind that in John's day people thought that prophecy was rare and prophets were rarer. Most people believed that the arrival of true prophets in the wilderness prefigured the coming of God's kingdom. Thus when John the Baptist began prophesying in the wilderness about God's coming kingdom, people began to stream out to him from across the land. Because John was dressed like Elijah of old (Matt. 3:4; 2 Kings 1:8), many of his followers probably considered him to be a new Elijah. The prophets had, after all, promised that Elijah would return just before the time of the end (Mal. 4:5–6). John's diet also showed that he was serious about his mission (Matt. 3:4). While some other Jewish people also ate locusts, a diet completely restricted to bugs and natural sweetener showed serious commitment!

Of course, John did not have a lot of choice about his diet or location; outspoken prophets are rarely welcome within established society. When true prophets like John begin to speak in modern society, we usually chase them out just like our ancient counterparts did. (Imagine how we might react if a prophet overturned the communion table in church Sunday morning and asked us how we could claim to be disciples of Christ when we are so materialistic, or how we could partake of "Christ's body" while attending a racially segregated church.)

Observing the crowds (Matthew zeroes in on the religious leaders who had come to check him out), John pleasantly called them "offspring of vipers" (Matt. 3:7), a nastier insult than modern readers might suspect. In John's day legends taught that vipers ate their way out of their mother's wombs, killing their mothers. Since ancient people considered parent-murderers the most morally reprobate people possible, calling someone the child of a viper was even worse than calling them a viper. Undoubtedly the religious people were not amused, but John did not stop with that insult. The religious folk then, like most religious people today, felt secure in their salvation. Jewish people generally thought they were saved because they were descended from Abraham (Matt. 3:9). But John warned them that only genuine repentance would spare them from the coming wrath (Matt. 3:7–8).

Rather than leaving "coming wrath" ambiguous, John explained to his hearers just what kind of wrath they could expect. He compared them to trees and warned that if they neglected the fruit of repentance, they would be cut down and hurled into the fire of judgment (Matt. 3:10). The coming one will gather his wheat into the barn, but he will burn up the chaff with unquenchable fire (Matt. 3:12). When farmers harvested wheat, they would hurl the wheat into the air, allowing the wind to blow out the chaff, a light substance that was useful only as cheap fuel that burned quickly. John told his hearers that those who had not repented and produced the behavioral fruit of repentance would be cast into a fire that never ceases to burn— the fire of hell.

This is the context of John's prophecy concerning being baptized in the Holy Spirit. The promised time of the kingdom and the restoration of Israel was coming (Matt. 3:2). God was preparing to gather his servants, but to burn up the wicked with fire. Whatever "fire" may symbolize in some other biblical texts, in this context it unquestionably symbolizes judgment (Matt. 3:10, 12). When John announced that the coming one would baptize in both the Holy Spirit and fire, his announcement was not entirely good news. In this context, baptism in fire can only be a negative promise of baptism in judgment for the wicked, whereas baptism in the Spirit is a positive promise for the righteous. (My students sometimes lament that this means that the whole "Fire-Baptized Holiness Church" is misnamed. But even if their name suggests a misinterpretation of this text, we know what they mean. We all affirm the importance of holiness.)

What did John mean by "baptism" in the Holy Spirit? Undoubtedly he was thinking of the Old Testament prophecies about God "pouring out" his Spirit on his people like water. Thus he would have thought of both prophetic empowerment, as in Joel and probably Isaiah, and purification, as in Ezekiel. The former emphasis is related to what most Pentecostals (and the Book of Acts) seem to mean by the baptism in the Holy Spirit; the latter is related to what most Baptist and Reformed thinkers (and Paul) mean by Spirit baptism. But John's prophecy about the outpoured Spirit must at least include conversion, because he explicitly contrasts it with a baptism of judgment for the wicked.

Perhaps more importantly, baptism in the Spirit, like baptism in fire, was what we call an "eschatological" baptism—that is, an event that John believed belonged to the impending end of the age. He predicted a baptism in the Spirit that was as imminent as the kingdom and God's fiery wrath that he was proclaiming. John did not understand, of course, that Jesus would have a first and second coming; thus he had no idea that the kingdom would come in two stages (see his confusion in Matt. 11:2–3). But we can look back and understand that the King who will someday come to reign has already inaugurated his reign among us his followers, although that reign's beginnings seemed as obscure (compared to the future kingdom) as a mustard seed before growing into a huge plant (Mark 4:30–32).

We recognize, though John may not have, that different aspects of his prophecy were fulfilled at different times. In Jesus' first coming and through the Spirit he gives, Jesus' followers have tasted the power of the coming kingdom. This means that through us God's will should be done on earth as it is in heaven, because we who believe in Jesus now are already people of the future. Whereas most people define their identity in terms of their past or their present, the gospel summons believers to define their identity in terms of what they shall be, in terms of what God has called them to be. Empowered by the Spirit, we are to represent the future kingdom in the midst of the present evil age!

Jesus the Spirit Baptizer (Mark 1:7–13)

The Gospels describe not only John the Baptist's preaching, but also Jesus' response to that preaching. The Gospel of Mark offers us the most concise summary of this story because Mark includes the account in his introduction, and introductions need to be short and to the point. (See, for instance, the introduction to this book!) Thus Mark includes only the most relevant points and uses them to introduce the major themes of his Gospel.

Mark mentions the Spirit only six times in his Gospel, but three of these times are in his introduction. This suggests that the Spirit is considerably more important for Mark than one might guess from the few times he mentions the Spirit later. In his introduction Mark builds three successive, concise paragraphs around the Spirit: John announces the Spirit baptizer (Mark 1:8), the Spirit descends on Jesus (Mark 1:10), and the Spirit drives Jesus into the wilderness for conflict with the devil (Mark 1:12).

The progression of these three paragraphs means that the promised Spirit baptizer himself becomes the model for the Spirit-baptized life, and that the Spirit-baptized life is a life of victorious conflict with the devil's kingdom. The rest of Mark traces the continuing conflict: Jesus defeats the devil by healing the sick and freeing those possessed by demons. The devil in turn strikes at Jesus through the devil's religious and political agents. Jesus finally dies, but conquers death itself in the resurrection. This is the model for Spirit-filled existence: a Christian must be ready to display God's power, but also to pay the price of death for doing so. The Spirit who inspired the Scriptures (Mark 12:36) and empowered Jesus to do miraculous works that skeptics reviled (Mark 3:22–29) will also anoint Jesus' witnesses to speak his message in times of persecution (Mark 13:11).[4] Mark was charismatic, but he was quite different from the kind of charismatics today who emphasize only the blessings of serving God. Mark recognized that the Spirit empowers us to do exploits for God as well as to suffer for his honor. As in the Book of Acts, irrefutable signs of God's activity lead not only to conversions but to active hostility and persecution (for example, Acts 4:7; 5:16–18; 14:3–6).

The Spirit and the Present Future (Rom. 8)

In Romans 8 Paul provides a similar picture of the Spirit's ministry to believers: the Spirit has made us present participants in the future kingdom to show this world what God's world should be like. In the midst of severe hardships, the Spirit guarantees our future inheritance, the greater glory resulting from our testings (8:16–18). Because, as we've noted, early Jews and Christians regarded the Spirit as the mark of the future age, they understood what we often do not. They recognized that those who have the Spirit taste the powers of the coming age in advance (Heb. 6:4–5). The Spirit enables us to view our identity in terms of our destiny in Christ, rather than by how the world's pressures define us (1 Cor. 2:12–16).

In Romans 8, the Spirit of the future era joins the present suffering creation in groaning with birth pangs for that new era to come and causes us to do likewise (Rom. 8:22–23, 26). Thus God works our trials for our good; prayers by the Spirit allow him to conform us to the image of his Son and to prepare us for our role in the coming age (8:26–30). In short, the Spirit makes the present bearable by reminding us that we live on another plane because we belong to another world. We are here, not as citizens of this age, but as invaders called to be faithful to the Lord of the world to come.

Paul here speaks of the Spirit as the "firstfruits" (8:23). The offering of firstfruits marked the actual beginning of the harvest (Lev. 23:10). We who long anxiously for our Lord's return do not simply await a theoretical hope for the distant future; we await something we know beyond any shadow of a doubt, because we have already begun to experience the life of the coming world. Elsewhere Paul speaks of the Spirit as the "down payment" or "earnest" of our future inheritance (2 Cor. 1:22; 5:5; Eph. 1:13–14). Businesspeople in Paul's day used this very term to speak of the first installment, the initial payment on what was to come. God has advanced us part of our inheritance now, so we can experience the life of the Spirit, "eternal life," in this present age (John 3:16, 36). Some promises await Jesus' return, but God's presence and power in our lives right now should enable us to live like heaven's people on earth. Can you imagine how it would revolutionize the lives of believers and churches if we actually recognized and believed this reality?

Washed by the Spirit: John's Water Motif

Some texts plainly associate the Spirit with purification from sin at conversion. When Nicodemus comes to Jesus by night, Jesus informs him that he must be "born again" (John 3:3). While we understand today that Jesus referred to spiritual rebirth, a miraculous transformation of our character by God's Spirit, Nicodemus was not so sure. He assumed that Jesus must mean entering his mother's womb and being physically reborn (3:4). The alternative, taking Jesus spiritually, was simply unthinkable to him. The only kind of spiritual rebirth Nicodemus knew about was appropriate only for pagans, not for religious persons such as himself.

Jewish people had a tradition that a Gentile converting to Judaism needed to be baptized. When the Gentile came up from the water, Jewish teachers regarded the person "as a newborn child," different from before. Nicodemus, like the religious people John the Baptist excoriated, could not imagine that he needed such a baptism of repentance. So Jesus makes being "born again" more explicit: a person must be born "from water and from the Spirit." The "water" would immediately remind Nicodemus of the Jewish ceremony used for Gentiles being legally "reborn" as Jews. Undoubtedly Nicodemus was unhappy with the comparison, for Jesus was suggesting that he, a *teacher of Israel*, needed to repent in order to belong to the people of God!

But Jesus was not asking Nicodemus merely to be baptized in water according to the Jewish ritual, as embarrassing as that would have been for him. Jesus wanted Nicodemus to be born of *spiritual* water, to be *spiritually* converted. In Greek, the expression "from water and the Spirit" could also be translated, "from the water *of* the Spirit." Lest anyone doubt that this is the likely meaning here, we should note that later in this Gospel, Jesus uses water as a symbol for the Spirit (John 7:37–39). This symbolic use of water carries on the image in Ezekiel that was popular among some of Jesus' contemporaries (Ezek. 36:25–27). Thus Jesus goes on to speak simply of "that which is born from the Spirit" (John 3:6). Natural birth was quite inadequate unless supplemented by Spirit rebirth.

An implicit contrast between water and the Spirit carries throughout the whole Fourth Gospel. John the Baptist declares that whereas he baptizes merely with water, Jesus will baptize in the Holy Spirit (John 1:31–33). In Cana, Jesus honors a friend's need more highly than traditional Jewish water rituals. Although weddings typically lasted seven days, running out of wine at one's wedding was so humiliating that Jesus' friend would be the laughingstock of Cana for years to come. So Jesus has attendants fill with water six waterpots that had been reserved for the ceremony of purification (John 2:6). To transform that water into wine profaned the normally holy purpose of the pots as far as Jewish tradition was concerned, but Jesus did it anyway. He had higher priorities than honoring merely ritual uses of water.

In chapter 4, Jesus meets a sinful Samaritan woman. Jewish teachers considered it immoral to speak with women in public. They considered Samaritan women unclean from the cradle, and of course everyone knew that a woman forced to come to the well alone was isolated from other women because of her sinful behavior. Jesus thus crosses at least three barriers to speak with the woman; consequently, she initially misinterprets him: "I'm not married," she suggests (John 4:17). But she eventually not only comes to faith but leads her people to Jesus as well (4:28–42). Jacob's well, water holy to the Samaritans, forms the backdrop for this story. It represents another side to religious ritual: ancient peoples often felt one could meet God only in special holy sites. (If this sounds superstitious to us today, we should remember how many nominal Christians similarly seek to meet God in church on Sunday mornings after they have spent no time with him during the week.) Jesus is greater than Jacob and greater than Jacob's well; he gives the water of eternal life, the Spirit (4:14).

Jesus is also superior to the water of ancient healing shrines. Some evidence suggests that the pool of Bethesda may have functioned as a healing shrine even after the destruction of Jerusalem, but one lame man at the pool had failed for thirty-eight long years to find healing there. Jesus, by contrast, provided healing instantly (John 5:5–9). John compares and contrasts this man with another whom Jesus healed by a pool in John 9. In that case, the pool is the Pool of Siloam, which had been used for special rituals during the Feast of Tabernacles just then ending. For the first seven days of the feast, priests would march in procession from the Pool of Siloam to the temple. On the eighth day they would recite ancient prophecies that someday rivers of living water would flow from the foundation stone of the temple, bringing life to all the earth (Ezek. 47:1–6; Zech. 14:8).

On the last day of the Feast of Tabernacles Jesus stood in the midst of the assembly in the temple and called out a promise of the Spirit to those who were listening (John 7:37–39). The earliest Greek text of this passage included no punctuation, so scholars are divided over how to punctuate the text. Many follow the traditional English reading: "Let whoever is thirsty come to me and drink. Of the one who believes in me, the Bible says, 'From his innermost being rivers of living water will flow'" (John 7:37–38). The NRSV even reads this view into the text: "out of the believer's heart." But in this context, I think that the other ancient view concerning the punctuation is probably more likely: "Whoever thirsts, let him come to me; let him drink, whoever believes in me. As the Bible says, 'From His innermost being rivers of living water will flow.'" The difference is that the latter punctuation helps us to see that Jesus himself is the foundation stone of a new temple, the source of living water for the believer. A believer may have a well of water springing up inside (4:14), but Jesus is the source of living water, and this text says that those who believe in him would receive the Spirit, not give it (John 7:39).

John informs us that the Spirit could not be given until Jesus was glorified (John 7:39)—that is, until he was "lifted up" on the cross (John 12:23–25, 32–33; see also 8:28; 17:1–5). After Jesus had died on the cross, John describes an event that the other Gospels do not report, because this event had special significance for his readers. When a soldier pierced Jesus' side with a spear, not only blood but water flowed out (19:34). Whatever the medical reasons for the water, John also urges on us a symbolic point in view of his illustrations about water elsewhere in his Gospel: the water from Jesus' side represents the gift of the Spirit, finally available after Jesus' death. From the throne of God and of the lamb flows the fountain of the river of life; let the one who wills come and drink freely (Rev. 22:1, 17).

Jesus gives the Spirit like living water to his people, a gift that we embrace at conversion (John 4:13–14; see also 1 Cor. 12:13) but that continues to flow like the fresh water of a river (John 7:37–38). True partakers of eternal life are those who continue to eat and drink of Christ (John 6:53–71; compare 8:31 with 8:59). Jesus promised that after he went to the Father, the Spirit would continue to empower his disciples both to understand his message (John 14:26; 16:12–15) and to witness (John

15:26–16:11). Because John is going to end his Gospel before the ascension, he cannot include Pentecost. Thus he must emphasize the way this promise of the Spirit began to be fulfilled already shortly after the resurrection. He therefore includes an incident shortly after Jesus rose from the dead when Jesus came to impart his Spirit to his disciples, breathing on them as God first breathed the breath of life into Adam (John 20:22; Gen. 2:7; see John 3:8; Job 27:3; Isa. 32:15; Ezek. 37:5–14). Thus the disciples were "born anew" with new life and were also equipped for mission: "As the Father sent me, I have sent you" (John 20:21).

The Power of Pentecost (Acts 2)

John 20:19–23 has to serve the basic purpose of Pentecost as far as John's Gospel is concerned, because of where John concludes. But Luke provides a fuller version of a complete empowerment by the Spirit that happened some time later. Yet Luke focuses on a single feature of that empowerment. Whereas John the Baptist, Paul, John the apostle, and others in the New Testament usually spoke of baptism in the Spirit as the whole sphere of the Spirit's work (including rebirth and prophetic inspiration), Luke focuses almost exclusively on the prophetic empowerment dimension of the Spirit. As many of us have argued elsewhere, Luke emphasizes particularly the Spirit's role in inspired speech (see Luke 1:15–17, 41–42, 67; 2:26; 12:12; Acts 1:2, 8; 2:4, 17; 4:8, 31; 5:32; 6:10; 7:51; 10:45–46; 11:28; 13:2, 4, 9; 20:23; 21:4, 11; compare 7:55; 8:29; 10:19, 38; 15:28; 16:6–9). By retaining John's contrast between Spirit and fire, Luke 3:16 may constitute the one clear exception to this emphasis. The portrait of Jesus in the Gospel of Luke serves later as the model for Spirit-empowered ministry in Acts. Among other parallels, just as Jesus' announcement of his Spirit-anointing in Luke 4:18–19 is programmatic for the Gospel of Luke, Acts 1:8 and 2:16–21 are programmatic for Acts.[5] Acts 2 is significant for any examination of New Testament teaching concerning the Spirit.

First, Luke surveys the *promise of Pentecost* (Acts 1:4–8). This special prophetic empowerment was so essential that Jesus commanded his disciples to wait in Jerusalem until it came (Luke 24:49; Acts 1:4–5). Because Jesus' contemporaries associated the Spirit especially with the end time, his disciples' response should not surprise us (see Isa. 44:3; Ezek. 36:24–28; 37:14; 39:29; Joel 2:27–3:1). When the disciples hear about the Spirit, they naturally expect that he is about to restore the kingdom to Israel. After all, the Messiah has come, the resurrection has begun (with Jesus), and the Spirit is about to be poured out; so the end time must be arriving (Acts 1:6–7). In words reminiscent of Isaiah's promise that Israel's remnant would become his witnesses to the nations, Jesus explains that the Spirit will empower his followers to carry their eyewitness testimony about him to all nations (1:8). This promise provides a rough outline for the expansion of the church in Acts: Jerusalem, Judea, Samaria, and on to the ends of the earth. (Specific summary statements divide Acts even more neatly: 6:7; 9:31; 12:24; 16:5; 19:20; 28:31.)

Second, Luke offers the *proofs of Pentecost* (Acts 2:1–4). Some Jews thought that Pentecost was the day that Moses had ascended Mount Sinai to receive the law. Some scholars thus draw a parallel between Moses' ascent and Jesus' ascension. But whether or not such a connection may be in the back of Luke's mind, it is not his main point. Clearer in the text are the signs of Pentecost: wind, fire, and tongues-speaking. To the early Christians, the wind would probably recall Ezekiel 37: in the end time, God would send a mighty wind of his Spirit to resurrect Israel. The fire might remind them of John's prophecy as well as Old Testament prophecies of end-time judgment (Luke 3:9, 16–17, for example, might be a reminder of Isa. 66:15–16 or Zeph. 1:18; 3:8). The empowerment to speak in languages they do not understand reminds them of the Old Testament promise of end-time prophetic enablement, as Peter goes on to make clear (Acts 2:16–18; Joel 2:28–29). These three signs constitute decisive proofs to the gathered Christians that many of the events of the end time are now taking place: the Messiah has been enthroned at God's right hand to rule until his enemies become his footstool (Acts 2:34–35; Ps. 110:1).

Third, Luke surveys the *peoples of Pentecost* (Acts 2:5–13). In a work that will emphasize God's agenda to reach all nations with the gospel (Acts 11:17–18), the initial empowerment to preach to foreign Jews from around the world provides a foretaste of the Christian mission in Acts. Some scholars think the list of nations here resembles astrological lists of the day; others more plausibly find Luke updating an Old Testament list of nations and implying a reversal of the curse of Babel. In any case, God shows his plan for "all flesh" even from the start (2:17), though the Twelve do not initially catch on until the seven bicultural ministers they appoint in chapter 6 begin to pave the way (8:4, 25). As early as chapters 1 and 2, the Book of Acts emphasizes that multiculturalism is God's idea (compare Rev. 5:9–10; 7:9), though it should also not surprise us if the world often perverts the idea to their own ends (Rev. 13:7, 16; Luke 2:1).

Fourth, Luke reminds us of the *prophecy of Pentecost* (Acts 2:14–21). Joel said God would pour out his Spirit "afterward" (Joel 2:28). Knowing Joel's context, Peter emphasized that this means "in the last days" (Acts 2:17; see Joel 3:1). What did all the tongues-speaking mean? many of the bystanders asked (Acts 2:12–13, 15–16). Peter replied that this tongues-speaking meant God was inspiring his servants to speak for him as the prophets did (Acts 2:17–18). If one can praise God in a language one does not know, one can surely be sensitive enough to the Spirit to prophesy or witness in a language one does know. Visions and dreams were typically prophetic activity (2:17), but just so no one misses the point that Peter refers to the Spirit of prophecy, he adds an explanatory line in his quotation of Joel: "and they shall prophesy" (2:18).

Fifth, Luke reports Peter's *preaching of Pentecost* (Acts 2:22–41). If the Spirit was being poured out, then the rest of Joel's prophecy was also true: they were in the end time, the era of salvation (2:21). Following a typical Jewish method of preaching, Peter breaks off his quote from Joel here and picks part of it up at the end of his sermon ("as many as the Lord our God shall call," 2:39). This means that he will be preaching on the last line quoted: "Whoever calls on the name of the Lord will be saved." In Joel, the "Lord" is God himself; but Jewish people in Peter's day did not like to pronounce God's name. By citing various passages that identify the Lord with the risen and reigning king, Peter explains that the name of the Lord on whom they are to call is Jesus of Nazareth, God in the flesh.

When Peter calls for a public commitment, he does not ask them to bow their heads and close their eyes to call on Jesus. As a friend of mine puts it, he wanted them "altered"—changed— not just "altared" (as in our modern altar calls that presume people will find it too embarrassing to accept Christ publicly). Referring to the many pools on the temple mount, Peter summoned his hearers to turn from sin and be baptized as followers of Jesus Christ (2:38).[6]

Finally, Luke depicts the true *power of Pentecost* (2:42–47). Prophetic empowerment was an initial expression of the Spirit's coming, but the long-range impact of Pentecost was the growth of the church and a community of believers who cared for one another in sacrificial ways. This paragraph provides the climax and focus of the Pentecost chapter: the Spirit's coming produces gifts, but especially produces fruit. The life of the Spirit in this passage contrasts starkly with the petty spiritual rivalries in many local churches today, even though some of them claim to be bearers of the Spirit. The work of the Spirit must go deeper than Spirit-led utterances and initial experiences alone.

The Power of Elijah for the Church

One who is familiar with the Old Testament need only read Luke's narratives about Jesus' miracles briefly to realize that the closest Old Testament parallels available for most of them are the stories about Elijah and Elisha. Although Elijah and Elisha probably used Moses as a model for some of their miracles, these prophets did not "lead" all God's people as Moses did, and both of them (especially Elijah) lived in a period when Israel's rulers were basically hostile to their message. Thus while some aspects of Jesus' ministry resemble Moses, many of his miracles resemble those of Elijah and Elisha, prophets during Israel's monarchy.

Elijah as a Model for Jesus and the Church

Clearly Jesus is not Elijah, though Elijah served as a model for Jesus and the church. John the Baptist functioned like the promised Elijah in one sense—as Jesus' forerunner (Luke 1:17); further, the literal Elijah, like Moses, is plainly subject to Jesus (Luke 9:30). Nevertheless, most of Jesus' miracles are more like those of Elijah and Elisha than like those of other Old Testament prophets. Like Elijah, he raises a widow's son (Luke 7:11–17; 1 Kings 17:17–24; compare 2 Kings 4:32–37); like Elijah and Elisha, Jesus multiplies food (Luke 9:10–17; 1 Kings 17:13–16; 2 Kings 4:42–44). By speaking of a prospective disciple's "plow" Jesus even alludes to the account of Elijah's call of Elisha, emphasizing that his own demands for discipleship are greater than Elijah's were (Luke 9:61–62; 1 Kings 19:19–21). Perhaps most significantly, Jesus' opening declaration compares his mission to the disenfranchised—ultimately to the Gentiles—with the ministries of Elijah and Elisha (Luke 4:24–27).

Many writers have pointed to the clear connections between Luke's Gospel and the Book of Acts, which constitute volumes one and two of Luke's history of the early Christian mission.[7] In volume two, Peter (the leading representative of Jewish Christianity) and Paul (the leading minister to early Gentile Christians) repeat many of Jesus' same miracles, showing how the church must carry on his mission in various cultures. Some commentators even think that Acts 1:1 summarizes Jesus' earthly mission as "all that Jesus *began* to do and to teach" because Luke recognizes that Jesus continues to perform his works through his church. Luke's Gospel closes and Acts opens with Jesus commissioning his church for a worldwide mission, empowered by the Spirit, until his return (Luke 24:47–49; Acts 1:8). As Elijah's mantle fell on Elisha and as other prophetic disciples sought to emulate their mentors, so the ascending Jesus empowered his church with the Spirit to carry on his mission to the ends of the earth.

As an exegete, I must try to understand what Scripture calls us to, even if it differs from my own experience. Although I hear reports of similar events from elsewhere, I myself rarely witness miracles on the scale of Elijah, Elisha, the Gospels, or Acts; and I confess that it might be easy for me to be a cessationist when it comes to such dramatic miracles. But my desire is to learn what Scripture teaches and then to seek to bring my life and the church's life into line with that norm. We do not need miracles just to prove to ourselves that we are spiritual, but we may need them to accomplish the sort of mission that Elijah and similar prophets undertook.

For power like Elijah's to be active in today's church does not mean that all believers would exercise miracles like Elijah's. John the Baptist, who like Elisha (2 Kings 2:9, 15) came "in the Spirit and power of Elijah" (Luke 1:17), preached God's message of repentance boldly and introduced the Messiah; but he performed no miracles (John 10:41). Different members of Christ's body have different gifts (1 Cor. 12:4–30). The church as a whole, through some of its members (usually especially apostles and prophets), must reappropriate these particular gifts. Further, God works in different ways in different times, according to the needs of that time. For example, God specially gifted Joseph and Daniel with dream interpretation, perhaps because they would serve in pagan courts where dream interpretation flourished. We should also remember that, though God rewarded the desperate faith of those seeking urgent miracles from him, the *maturest* faith appears in a deep relationship with God. Such a faith-relationship is developed over time as we persevere through trials (for example, Heb. 11:8–19, 23–29, 35–38). Nevertheless, significant aspects of Elijah's ministry remain a model of Spirit-empowered ministry for the church as a whole and, in many respects, for individual believers as well.

Thus, while exhorting believers that a righteous person's prayer for healing will be effective (James 5:14–16), James reminds us that Elijah was a person "of like passions" as we are (5:17–18). If God heard Elijah when he requested drought or rain, the text declares, we who also serve God can trust Him to hear our prayers.

One morning our campus ministry had scheduled a march in Livingstone College's homecoming parade, but we feared that the downpour outside was going to "dampen" our witness. So Sharon Wells, a student from the chapter of New Generation Campus Ministries at North Carolina A & T State University, decided to lead us in prayer for the rain to stop. It couldn't hurt, I thought, though the college administration was at that moment in the process of calling off the parade. No sooner had Sharon prayed than the rain became like the dripping of a faucet just turned off. Within a few minutes the rain had stopped entirely, and it did not rain again that day. I marveled at the faith of the students eager to witness, who did not pause to doubt whether God could control the rain. When James makes Elijah's faith a model for ours, why *shouldn't* we be able to trust God for miracles? The Holy Spirit gives us boldness to ask for things in accordance with God's will because we walk in his desires for his work in the world rather than our own agendas (1 John 3:21–24; 5:14–15).

One more text may support the use of Elijah as a model for the church's ministry. Although any suggestion on the Book of Revelation will be controversial, I suspect that Revelation 11:3–6 may portray God's church as experiencing the kind of miraculous power exhibited in the ministries of Moses and Elijah. The angel describes two witnesses to John in language taken from Zechariah 4:2–3, where the words refer to a king and a priest leading God's work in Zechariah's day (Zech. 3:6–9; 4:6–14). In Revelation, however, all God's people are a kingdom and priests (1:6; 5:10; see Exod. 19:6). Further, by calling these witnesses "lampstands" (11:4) Revelation may suggest that they symbolize the church (1:20, though see also Zech. 4:2, 11). If this suggestion is correct, the church performs miracles like Moses and Elijah in Revelation 11:6. Whether one concurs with this interpretation will depend largely on how one reads the Book of Revelation as a whole, but those who do agree would find here another case in which New Testament writers saw Elijah as a model for the church.

Practical Implications of Elijah's Model

The biblical portrayal of Elijah and Elisha challenges us in a variety of ways. Although Elijah and Elisha were miracle-workers, they hardly look like many modern "prosperity" preachers who claim miraculous power. God provided for Elijah, but eating from ravens' mouths and drinking from a brook (1 Kings 17:4) is hardly luxury. In response to Gehazi's pursuit of moderate resources, Elisha explicitly repudiated the valuing of material possessions (2 Kings 5:26–27). Moreover, Elijah's ministry required him to confront hostile officials, to live outside the confines of his own society, and to risk death for the honor of the One who had called him (1 Kings 17–19). Unlike many, probably most, other prophets (Num. 12:1; 1 Kings 13:11; 2 Kings

4:1; Isa. 8:3; Ezek. 24:18)—but like Jeremiah (Jer. 16:2–4), John, Jesus, and Paul—the call of Elijah and Elisha apparently forced them to remain unmarried.

That Jesus calls us as disciples to even costlier commitment than Old Testament prophets (Luke 9:61–62; compare 1 Kings 19:19–21) indicates the seriousness of his call. A Spirit-filled life like Elijah's or Elisha's does not mean homelessness in all circumstances (according to 2 Kings 5:9 Elisha had a house), but it does mean that we must value nothing so much that we cannot readily surrender it for God's call. I suspect that too many of us, for all our claims to be people of the Spirit, are so in love with our worldly possessions and pursuits that if God *is* calling us to give them up we cannot hear him.

Lest we think Elijah too holy to provide a model for us, we must also pause to remember that Elijah was human in the same way we are (James 5:17). This is not to deny that Elijah was exercising a faith nurtured by years of an intimate relationship with God, but this faith depended on God's power, not Elijah's (compare Acts 3:12–13). Elijah dared work his miracles only at God's command (1 Kings 18:36). Presumptuously seeking to work miracles on one's own will lead only to public embarrassment for oneself and God's people (compare Lam. 3:37–38), and one who has not learned sensitivity to God's Spirit should not step out on presumption. Had Elijah himself been calling the shots, he undoubtedly would have gotten his food somewhere besides ravens, but Elijah's authority came only from God's commission. Unlike some of us, Elijah was forced to remember that he was God's servant, empowered only to do God's will.

But Elijah was so confident that God had spoken that he was extravagant in proving that the fire would have to be a miracle. Although water was a rare commodity in this time of drought, he had the people pour water around the altar (1 Kings 18:33–35). After the miracle, Elijah was able to take vengeance on the prophets of Baal for the blood of his fellow prophets

(18:40), many of whom may have been Elijah's own disciples (compare 18:13).

Yet despite what appeared to be an initial turning of the people to God, Elijah's feeling of climactic success was short lived. Jezebel was neither persuaded nor weakened in her throne but forced Elijah to become a refugee again (1 Kings 19:1–2). Fire from heaven should have brought Israel to revival, but instead it simply seemed to increase the opposition. Many of us have labored in God's work and finally seen the fruit of our labors, only to experience what seem insurmountable setbacks. Elijah, who was a person of flesh and blood just like us, became discouraged (19:3–5).

Once we realize that the power and the orders come from God rather than from ourselves, we will be ready for God to send us and use us the way he sees fit. We should pray for God to grant signs to his church for its work of evangelism; we should also be ready for the life of faith God asks of each of us—with signs, suffering, and finding sufficiency in him alone. The ultimate objective goes beyond signs, and even beyond evangelism and church growth; the goal to which these other activities lead is presenting people who are mature in Christ (Col. 1:28). Although God will not empower most of us with the same gifts to the same degree that he empowered Elijah, all of us may learn from Elijah's example of faith, perseverance, and faithfulness. We may also pray for God to raise up men and women of God with that kind of faith and power for our generation.

Satan does not mind trotting forth his power. If the world is to recognize that God's power is greater, God's representatives must start believing it and acting accordingly.[8] During my first year in college, I was preaching at a street mission when a demon-possessed man began shouting that he was "Antichrist" and "Lucifer" (leave it to a demon to take Scripture out of context, as the titles implied he was doing). I had assumed that I was spiritually prepared to cast a demon out, but remembering the story of the seven sons of Sceva, I was too scared to attempt it. Other workers escorted the man out, and I finished my sermon as best I could. Ashamed at my failure, I realized that most of the "demons" I'd tried to cast out in prayer previously weren't real demons at all and that I did not have enough faith for the real thing. I resolved to become a stronger man of faith, and some months later I was tested again.

This time I was visiting a recently converted widow whose daughter was experiencing some serious problems. As I was praying for them outside, the Spirit suddenly led me back into the house to a door that opened to a stairwell, and down the stairs toward another door in the basement. I found myself unable to reach that door, however. An evil presence radiated menacingly from that room, almost like it was the ghost of the widow's husband. Knowing that "ghosts" are merely demons impersonating deceased people, I prayed upstairs and then marched down the stairs, my strength renewed. I threw open the door and in Jesus' name commanded the spirit to depart, never to return. Instantly it was gone. As I rejoined the widow, she informed me of three matters I hadn't known: (1) the basement room was directly beneath her daughter's bedroom; (2) her former husband had been involved with the occult, and his belongings were stored in that room; and (3) a man she had dated a year before, who claimed to have psychic powers, had tried to confront the "ghost" of her husband in that room, but it had chased him away.

Although I prefer to share my own, firsthand testimonies (because I know more of them), many others who are involved in frontline evangelism have far more dramatic accounts of the need for the Spirit's power. Given what we are up against in our cities and elsewhere today, I am convinced that nothing short of such radical faith will allow us to evangelize the "hard" areas. Yet as much as we need Elijahs, the church as a whole may currently need more prophets like Jeremiah (who worked no signs, but called for repentance in the face of impending judgment) to shake us from our complacency about God's mission in the world. Let us pray that God's Spirit will give us the various voices we need most to reach our generation for Christ.

One, Two, or More Works of Grace?

As noted earlier, many Christians in the Wesleyan, Holiness, and Pentecostal traditions have argued for a second work of grace that frequently occurs after conversion. In such circles, the work can be viewed as "sanctification" or "baptism in the Holy Spirit." Some groups also distinguish between sanctification and Spirit baptism, thus providing three works of grace. With some notable exceptions (such as many Puritan writers), the Reformed tradition normally argues that one receives everything at conversion. In this chapter we argue that both traditions are largely correct in what they affirm. Most Christians might, in fact, agree on the basic issues if we could get past semantics: the Spirit transforms us at conversion, but God can subsequently fill Christians with the Spirit in special ways and for special tasks.

The experience of genuine empowerment is probably more important than the semantics, but the disagreement on terminology stems primarily from the different ways the New Testament writers themselves speak about the Spirit. Because of the variety in the Spirit's work, Paul may refer to one aspect of the Spirit's work by the phrase "receiving the Spirit," while Luke may use the same phrase to refer to a different aspect.

Paul's Theology of the Spirit

Paul is absolutely clear that one receives all of Christ's provision at conversion. Those who try to add to the finished work of Christ, whether they be circumcizers in Galatia or mystics in Colosse, undermine the gospel itself. At conversion we were "sealed" in Christ for the day of redemption (Eph.

4:30); those who do not have the Spirit are simply not Christians at all (Rom. 8:9).

Some Christians who dispute this conclusion have tried to argue that "sealing" with the Spirit in Ephesians 1:13 occurs *after* believing the gospel, for the verb tense used here usually implies subsequence. The problem with this argument is that it focuses on grammar rather than on context and the writer's style; exceptions to this typical grammatical principle are abundant. Only a few verses later, where Paul uses the same construction, it cannot imply subsequence because if it did, it would mean that God exerted his mighty power in Christ *after* resurrecting him, rather than *by* resurrecting him (Eph. 1:19–20; compare Rom. 1:4). More importantly, the text indicates that this seal of the Spirit is a down payment guaranteeing our future inheritance at the redemption of our bodies (Eph. 1:13–14). If this sealing is *subsequent* to conversion, then conversion is inadequate to guarantee us a place in God's kingdom. We were sealed by the Spirit "for the day of redemption" (Eph. 4:30).

Paul is no less clear in other texts about receiving the Spirit. Whatever Luke means when he speaks of disciples "receiving the Spirit" (see below), Paul clearly means conversion. The Galatians want to earn their spiritual experience by coming up to the cultural standards of law-keeping Jewish-Christian missionaries. Thus Paul emphasizes that they "received the Spirit" by faith, not by obeying the law (Gal. 3:2; compare 1 Cor. 2:12). The Spirit always comes as a gift rather than as something we earn (Rom. 5:5). Even in Ephesians 5:18, the command to be "filled with the Spirit" is passive, suggesting receptivity to divine action. If that was true of the *beginning* of their life in the Spirit (conversion), how could the Galatian Christians possibly hope to *complete* their Christian life by legalistic works (Gal. 3:3)? In 1 Corinthians, Paul divides humanity into two groups: those who have the Spirit ("spiritual") and those who do not ("fleshly," or "natural"; 2:10–16). Of course the finished work of Christ does not *force* us to live according to the Spirit. Even though the Corinthian Christians were Spirit-people by virtue of their conversion (1 Cor. 6:11), by dividing and competing spiritually they were acting like the world. Paul uses two expressions: one meaning "flesh*like*," the other meaning "as *if* you were fleshly" (1 Cor. 3:1–3).

Romans 8, which mentions the Spirit of God more than any other chapter in the Bible, makes the same point. To counter some Jewish Christians' view that the law gave them a spiritual advantage, Paul insists that he too had once lived life under the law. Yet whereas most Jewish teachers felt that the law empowered people to overcome the evil impulse within them, Paul declared that for him it simply brought evil more into focus, until it controlled him. One could not achieve righteousness by depending on one's ability to fulfill the law. One died to sin only through Christ—through accepting the finished work of Christ and continually reaffirming it by faith (Rom. 6:1–11). Under the law, Paul said, he found that he was "fleshly," "sold into slavery to sin" (7:14). In Christ, however, he was "not in the flesh" (8:9) but had been redeemed from slavery to sin (6:18, 20, 22). No longer was the law simply a death sentence. Now, written in the believer's heart, the law was the moral guidance of God's own Spirit (8:2; compare Jer. 31:33–34; Ezek. 36:26–27).

No longer would sin dwelling in the person control the person (Rom. 7:17–18). Now the Spirit lives in the believer, and any professed believer who does not have this Spirit does not belong to Christ (8:9). In the subsequent context, Paul borrows images relating to the time when God first saved his people Israel and applies these images to Christians: like Israel, we "groan" because of our slavery (Exod. 2:23; Rom. 8:23); God has begun to free us from that bondage (Exod. 2:24; Rom. 8:15); God has adopted us as his children (Exod. 4:22; Rom. 8:14–16); he leads us on our way in the present time (Exod. 13:21; Rom. 8:14); and he has a future inheritance for us (Num. 33:53–54; Rom. 8:17), so that the fulfilment of our redemption awaits that future promised inheritance (Rom. 8:23). From start to finish, Christians are people whose future hope is guaranteed by God's Spirit within them (Rom. 8:9–11, 14–16, 23, 26–27), just as God's presence with Israel was their guarantee of victory. Clearly anyone who does not have the Spirit in the Romans 8 sense is not yet saved. And if Paul believes in receiving the Spirit as a second work distinct from this work, he gives not the slightest clue here or anywhere else in his writings.

At the same time, Paul recognizes that believers can avail themselves of a continued "supply" of the Holy Spirit (Phil. 1:19).[9] He summons them to "remain filled with the Spirit" continuously (Eph. 5:18), and he expects them to walk in the Spirit and produce the fruit of the Spirit (Gal. 5:16–23)—a matter on which he exhorts them precisely because they were falling short. Perhaps his view that God continues to "give" (present tense) his Spirit to the Galatians also implies a continuing supply of God's power (Gal. 3:5). Although it could refer to the continuing experience of welcoming newcomers into the community, Paul nowhere else in the letter has newcomers in view. In other words, although all God's fullness becomes ours in Christ at the moment of our conversion, we still have to actualize that fullness in our daily lives. By way of analogy, it is one thing to be dead to sin in Christ—that is accomplished at conversion (Rom. 6:3–4; Col. 3:3); it is quite another to *live* like we are dead to sin (Rom. 6:11–14; 8:13; Col. 3:5). Any Christian who has sinned since his or her conversion recognizes this difference. Likewise, any Christian who has faltered in his or her witness or sensitivity to God's leading recognizes the need for a greater dependence on the Spirit's power, to which God has given us full access in Christ.

Acts and Christian Experience of the Spirit

When God's Spirit inspired the Bible through chosen people obedient to his leading (Rom. 1:2), he worked through their distinctive styles and modes of expression. That is why Isaiah reads different from Jeremiah, Jeremiah from Ezekiel, and so on. God even had a special nickname for Ezekiel—"son of man," or "human one"—which he did not apply to most of his prophets. This is one reason we dare not jump to the conclusion that a particular phrase means the same thing in every passage or for every writer. Sometimes it plainly means something different. That is why James and Paul do not contradict each other even though they say very different things about faith; they are using their terms differently (Rom. 4:5; James 2:14). By "receiving the Spirit," John or Paul may refer to a particular aspect of the Spirit's work, while Luke may refer to a different one.

We noted earlier that Jewish people in the first century entertained different conceptions of the Holy Spirit. Whereas John and Paul blend these conceptions together (new birth and prophetic empowerment; compare 1 Sam. 10:6, 10), Luke's writings focus almost exclusively on prophetic empowerment. Thus being "filled with the Spirit" normally results in prophetic speech (Luke 1:15, 41–42, 67; Acts 2:4; 13:9–10) or witness (Acts 4:8, 31; only 9:17 lists no effects, and 13:52 alone appears to constitute an exception). Whereas one might think from Paul that baptism in the Spirit and receiving the Spirit occur at conversion (but filling afterward), Luke seems to identify this initial filling of the prophetic Spirit with the baptism in the Spirit (Acts 2:4 fulfills 1:4–5; see 2:33, 39) and "receiving the Spirit" (2:38–39). The Spirit could "come on" believers (as he came on the prophets of old) when they "received" him (10:44, 47; 19:2, 6), an experience identified with the Pentecost experience of the first disciples and called being "baptized in the Holy Spirit" (10:47; 11:15–17; note also the expression "poured out" in 10:45). Thus the Samaritans could be converted, yet not have "received the Spirit" in the sense in which Luke means the phrase (8:15–16; see discussion below).[10]

Even for Luke, however, conversion is the only prerequisite for "receiving the Spirit" (Acts 2:38). On the level of direct theological statements, Luke probably would have preached exactly the same message as Paul or John: you receive the Spirit when you accept Christ as Lord and Savior. But on the level of *experience*, some people encounter a fuller prophetic empowerment of the Spirit after conversion. We dare not underestimate the significance of Luke's testimony, because Acts is the *only* New Testament book that directly depicts early Christian experience (although we may infer other aspects of that experience from letters that address it). Rather than interpreting half of the examples in Acts in a way that harmonizes them with Paul, perhaps we need to look at Acts to understand how the New Testament's theological statements function in *practice*. Luke apparently intends us to interpret his direct statement in Acts 2:38 and his narrative examples in light of each other.

Examples of Receiving the Spirit in Acts

Sometimes the Spirit came at conversion, even in Acts. Although some have argued that Cornelius and his household (Acts 10) were believers before Peter preached, the evidence of the text argues otherwise. God sent Peter precisely so that these Gentiles could hear the gospel, believe, and be saved, having their hearts cleansed by faith (11:14; 15:7–11). Peter had earlier declared that all who repented and were baptized would receive the gift of the Spirit (2:38), and the conversion of Cornelius's household provides an almost textbook example of this promise. Hearing the gospel, they immediately were baptized in the Holy Spirit, even before they had received water baptism. (It was a good thing it happened this way, too, or Peter's companions may have wanted to circumcise them first!) Here the theology of the Spirit worked out in practice exactly as it did in theory: a person received the Spirit in his overwhelming fulness through faith at the moment of conversion.

Yet does the principle always work this easily in practice? Most Christians, for instance, do not experience an equally dramatic overwhelming of the Spirit at conversion as this text describes. The gospel declares that we died to sin when we accepted Christ, which means that the normal Christian life should be sinless. Yet most Christians I know did not begin living such normal Christian lives immediately at conversion, although deliverance from sin is implicit in our conversion. It is the standard we should look for, but we should not declare a conversion inauthentic if all its anticipated fruits do not sprout forth at once. Baptism in the Spirit may provide a similar example of delayed action.

Other examples of conversions in Acts which mention the Spirit's coming are not as simple as Acts 10. Some examples do not explicitly mention the Spirit at all, offering no evidence in either direction. In other cases, Luke notes only an encounter with the Spirit after conversion. Paul appears to have accepted Christ's lordship before being filled with the Spirit for the first time (9:17). In Acts 9:5 Paul acknowledges Jesus' identity. Some writers may overemphasize Paul's understanding of Jesus at this point, suggesting that his whole gospel was implicit in this revelation. Nevertheless, Paul apparently had at least made the basic acknowledgement necessary to be a Christian. Once he recognized that Jesus was Lord, he submitted himself to obey whatever Jesus said (Acts 9:5–6, 8; 22:10; 26:15–16). In contrast to what some writers suggest, Paul's "Lord" here hardly means merely "sir"; the character of Jesus' revelation to him was similar to Old Testament manifestations of God's glory and would leave Paul little doubt what Jesus' lordship actually involved.

True, Paul may not "officially" have been a Christian until his baptism (22:16), but this does not mean that he had not yet made his inward commitment to Christ. Jewish people had Gentiles "baptized" as an act of conversion to Judaism, so Jewish people would understand baptism as an act of conversion. This understanding should not suggest, however, that the Spirit waits to transform the repentant heart until water is applied to the body! The New Testament picture of baptism is like our contemporary engagement ring: a man may ask a woman to marry him, but usually she wants more than his request—she wants to see the *ring*. Baptism makes it official, as a public testimony of one's commitment to Christ, but baptism is the result of (rather than the cause of) one's inward commitment. If my understanding is correct (that is, if being a Baptist has not biased me on the baptism issue), Luke shows us that Paul had already submitted to Christ's call three days before being filled with the Spirit. Whether or not one agrees that Paul's faith in Christ preceded his empowerment by the Spirit, most readers would still agree that believers can be "filled" with the Spirit after conversion. It is the language of "receiving" the Spirit (which does not appear in this passage) that bothers some people.

Acts 19 speaks of "certain disciples" receiving the Spirit. "Disciples" refers to Christians elsewhere in Acts, including the description, "certain disciple(s)" (9:10, 36; 16:1), as classical Pentecostal scholars point out.[11] At the same time, these particular disciples had only received John's baptism and had not yet heard that the Holy Spirit had come, which suggests to me that they left Palestine before Pentecost and were not in fellowship with Christians. In other words, scholars who argue that these particular disciples were probably disciples of John, rather than Christians, are probably right. Nevertheless, they do not "receive the Spirit" in the Lukan sense at the exact moment of their fuller faith in Christ or their Christian baptism; they receive it afterward when Paul lays hands on them (19:6). Can we honestly suggest that these disciples had not been converted at least a few minutes before, and thus had to receive the Spirit in conversion through the laying on of hands? If that is what this text teaches, we would have to adjust the way we do altar calls in most of our Baptist churches! Conversion may involve a process, as some argue, but unless we believe in spiritual purgatory, surely faith and not the laying on of hands is the point at which one passes from spiritual death to spiritual life.

THE SAMARITANS IN ACTS 8

Acts 2 speaks of believers receiving the Spirit after they have already been following Christ, but many interpreters consider this example an exception. Although I suspect that Luke intends it in many respects as a *model* rather than as an exception, for the sake of argument I will turn instead to Acts 8, where people apparently are converted and then afterward "receive the Spirit." Some interpreters, like John MacArthur, consider Acts 8 another exception, due to the transitional period covered by Acts. But interpreters who treat examples of subsequence in Acts as exceptions should honestly acknowledge what their approach implies. If only reception of the Spirit at the moment of conversion (Acts 10) is normative, we must explain as exceptions instances where believers received the Spirit in some sense after conversion (anywhere from a few minutes to a few days; see Acts 2, 8, 9, and 19). When four of our five biblical examples are "exceptions," however, one is tempted to question the validity of the "rule."

Acts is history, but very few Acts scholars today would ignore that Luke teaches theology through his history, a fact that I. Howard Marshall, Charles Talbert, and Robert Tannehill among others have forcefully demonstrated (and one that Paul clearly indicates in 2 Tim. 3:16).

Luke does not treat all of early apostolic history (in one volume!), but emphasizes those features that advance the themes about which he must inform his audience. Given that ancient writers normally expected readers to draw morals from their narratives, the burden of proof rests on those who contend that Luke's history does *not* teach theology, rather than on those who contend that it does. Most of the events Luke reports are exceptional in some sense, narrating the carrying forth of the gospel (with the attendant Christian baptism and the gift of the Spirit) to different groups of people. But this hardly means that Luke wants us to think the patterns he establishes among different groups ceased in his own day. Rather, he wants us to recognize that this pattern follows all Christians regardless of their background. Being filled with the Spirit should be a normal part of all Christians' lives.

Acts presents Philip, like Stephen, in an unambiguously positive light (6:3–7; 8:4–5), for, unlike the apostles, he was ready to begin crossing cultural barriers from the start. The inhabitants of a leading Samaritan city, perhaps ancient Shechem, responded with joy to Philip's preaching and healing ministry (8:6–8). This kind of joyous response also characterized Paul's ministry (13:48, 52), although most of Paul's audiences also included hostile responses alongside the receptive ones. The description of signs and wonders sounds like those God worked through other of his servants in Acts (2:43; 3:6–7; 4:30; 5:12–16; 6:8; 14:3; 19:11–12). Philip was preaching "Christ" (8:5) and "the good news of God's kingdom" (8:12), just as Paul later did (20:25; 28:31). One would think that Philip understood the gospel, understood what was essential for conversion, and knew better than to baptize those who had not yet committed themselves to Christ.

The text also tells us that the Samaritans "believed" (8:12)—a term applied elsewhere in Acts to saving faith (for example, 4:4; 10:45; 11:17; 14:1–2; 15:7, 9; 16:1; 17:12, 34; 19:18), especially when accompanied by baptism, as here (16:31–34; 18:8). The text indicates that they believed "Philip proclaiming good news of the kingdom"; that is, they embraced the gospel.

Everywhere else in Acts where followers of Jesus offer baptism, it is because those being baptized have accepted the gospel (2:41; 9:18; 10:47; 16:33; 18:8; 19:5). They "accepted God's word" (8:14), language that throughout Acts normally refers to conversion (2:41; 11:1; compare 17:11). If these baptized believers who received God's message with joy were not converted, is anyone in the whole Book of Acts converted? "Repentance" seems to be assumed as part of faith and baptism; after 2:38 it is mentioned (11:18; 13:24; 14:15; 17:30; 20:21; 26:18), but rarely in descriptions of conversions. Baptism is often assumed in the term "believed," but here it is explicitly mentioned. Yet they still need to "receive" the Holy Spirit (8:15), although this is the same expression Acts 2:38 promised in response to conversion (10:47; 19:2). The promise was available upon conversion, but apparently had not yet been appropriated. Whether the early Christians regarded this delay as "normal" or not—the apostles do seem to have been concerned—a delay plainly is in view.[12]

Is there any other way to explain the postconversion reception of the Spirit in Acts 8? Indeed there is. James Dunn, whose excellent classic work on the New Testament teaching on the baptism in the Spirit is in most respects quite helpful, argues that the Samaritans were not genuinely converted. In contrast to many scholars before him, who suggested that the Samaritans must have received the Spirit earlier with the manifestation coming later (Calvin, Bruce, Beasley-Murray), or that this refers to a second reception of the Spirit (most Roman and Anglo-Catholics [for confirmation] and Pentecostals), Dunn contends that the Samaritans were not converted until, in effect, the Jerusalem apostles came to lay hands on them.[13] If Dunn's interpretation of this text provided a model for conversion, it would suggest an extraordinary precedent (one which, fortunately, Dunn himself does not draw): people may receive God's word with joy, may believe, may receive Christian baptism, yet may still require apostles to lay hands on them to complete their conversion. Worse yet, the text would call into question Luke's usual terminology for conversion and leave one wondering if faith in the gospel and baptism are sufficient. Dunn seeks to avoid this conclusion by presenting Luke's use of the terminology in Acts 8 as exceptional. But a survey of Luke's use of the terminology (below) indicates that the variations are too subtle for the average reader of Acts to catch them. Since most of Luke's first audience would have simply heard Acts read in church services, Dunn's overly subtle case would have surely eluded them. Instead, I believe that they would have read this text as Pentecostals do.

Dunn's thesis does not permit him to accept a postconversion experience with the Spirit here:

> The problem of Acts 8, long the chief stronghold of Pentecostal (baptism in the Spirit) and Catholic (Confirmation) alike, centres on two facts: the Samaritans believed and were baptized; they did not receive the Spirit until some time later. The problem is that in the context of the rest of the NT these facts appear to be mutually exclusive and wholly irreconcilable.[14]

But must one force the details of Acts 8 (as I believe Dunn does) to fit "the rest of the New Testament"? Or might a more plausible explanation exist? As Clark Pinnock puts it, referring to Dunn's own belief that various New Testament writers might articulate their message in different ways, "Ironically, at this point at least, there is greater diversity in the New Testament than even Jimmy Dunn is prepared to grant!"[15]

Dunn argues that the Samaritans' conversion was not genuine by appealing to what he thinks are special irregularities in the narrative.[16] He contends that Samaritans were superstitious and easily misled by magic. But ancient texts tell us the same about most other ancient peoples, not least the people of Ephesus (Acts

19:18–19). He further argues that the way the Samaritans "believe" here constitutes only intellectual assent, in contrast to saving faith, because Luke uses a Greek case called the dative. If this argument sounds strong to those who do not know Greek, one should keep in mind that Dunn provides only two examples of "believe" with this dative meaning, neither of which is clear. Luke *usually* employs the dative with "believe" when the object of faith is a person, with absolutely no indication that the faith is defective (for example, Acts 16:34; 18:8; 27:25). Because few "rules" in first-century Greek functioned without exception, arguments from grammar may be helpful but must always be examined carefully.

Further, apostolic baptism always presupposes faith in Christ (22:16), and the apostles accepted Philip's baptism of the believing Samaritans as legitimate. We know that the apostles accepted the Samaritans' baptism because, in contrast to Acts 19:5 (a defective baptism by John alone), they do not rebaptize the Samaritans.[17] Dunn is correct that Simon the Sorcerer's initial faith did not seem to prove as enduring as that of the Samaritans (8:18–24), but Luke (no less than the rest of the New Testament) requires perseverance as well as an initial profession of faith (whether to prove one's salvation, as some hold, or to keep it, as others hold). As Ervin points out, Simon proving a false or apostate convert tells us no more about the reality of the Samaritans' faith than Judas's apostasy tells us about that of the Twelve (Acts 1:17).

Gordon Fee, a Pentecostal scholar who does not differentiate Spirit baptism from conversion (regarding the former as the experiential dimension of the latter), also finds Dunn's case in Acts 8 weak. He thinks that the point in Acts 8 is not subsequence, which admittedly does not appear to be the ideal for the Christian experience. (Note that the apostles sought for the Samaritan converts to receive the Spirit as quickly as possible.) Rather, this passage emphasizes "the experiential, dynamic quality of the gift of the Spirit" which completes the conversion experience. Fee believes that the church in later centuries largely abandoned this experiential dimension of conversion through not expecting it. He is not implying that those who lack the experience are unconverted, but (if I have understood him correctly) that most Christians have settled for less than their spiritual birthright as Christians.[18]

My approach, which emphasizes prophetic empowerment more than an experiential dimension of conversion, is somewhat different from Fee's. Though Fee is correct that in Acts it was quite normal for Christians to experience the full working of the Spirit at conversion, in my view Acts 8 does allow that the experience of prophetic empowerment (implicitly available in conversion itself) may occur after conversion. (My own experience actually fits Fee's view as well as my own, but it does not fit that of most other committed Christians that I know. In the final analysis, of course, experience may be helpful but is not normative anyway.) In any case, however, much of the disagreement on the relation of "receiving the Spirit" (in the Lukan sense) to conversion is semantic. Unless one takes Dunn's view here, these Christians plainly *experienced* something that the apostles considered essential for Christians, and experienced it *after* conversion. Such delay may not have been the ideal either then or today, but Acts shows us real Christian experience, not just the theological ideal.

ONLY TWO EXPERIENCES IN ACTS?

While Christians in Acts sometimes entered this new sphere of spiritual experience shortly after conversion (Acts 8:14–17; 9:17; see also 1:4–5; 19:5–6), sometimes they experienced it during or almost simultaneous to their conversion (Acts 10:44; 11:14–15; 19:4–6). What may surprise us, however, is that Spirit-empowerment did not stop with what some call a "second work of grace," even among those who had undoubtedly received a full "dose" of the Spirit by that point. For example, Peter and John were unquestionably among those who received the Spirit on Pentecost (Acts 2:1–4, 14), but they later received additional power for a special circumstance, power reminiscent of God's Spirit "coming on" his prophets or other servants in ancient Israel (Acts 4:8; see Judg. 6:34; 13:25; 14:19; 1 Sam. 10:6; 19:20). Likewise, Paul was filled with the Spirit shortly after Acts 9:17, but God filled him anew for a special situation in Acts 13:9. (The terminology provides no clear distinction between the filling of 13:9 and what we might call his initial filling in 9:17 or the church's initial filling in 2:4.) Whole assemblies of people also experienced such outpourings of the Spirit in fervent prayer meetings (4:31 and 13:52). Other experiences with the Spirit undoubtedly occurred; Luke merely provides samples of the Spirit's works, usually encountered during prayer or ministry of the Word.

In other words, Acts, like Paul, is not simply calling us to a second (or third, or fourth) spiritual experience.[19] Acts is summoning us to a Spirit-empowered life, by whatever initial and continuing experiences we are introduced into it. Acts challenges many Pentecostals and charismatics who are satisfied to pray in tongues but neglect God's power in other ways (especially power for witness) no less than it challenges many non-Pentecostals who are satisfied with a static devotional life devoid of real passion or power. If my observations of today's church are accurate, I suspect that those most clearly experiencing God's power like that found in Acts are those living on the cutting edge of evangelism—Christians challenging the powers of darkness on their own turf by reaching unevangelized and often hostile people with the gospel. When those who are born of the Spirit enter crisis situations in obedience to God's call, they learn dependence on God's Spirit.

Second-work Pentecostals and their theological cousins in the Wesleyan and Holiness traditions have brought a gift to the rest of Christ's body by reminding us that we all need an experiential empowerment of the Spirit, just as other traditions have rightly emphasized the need to depend on the finished work of Christ. Whether we think of that empowerment as implicit in our conversion, in our water baptism, or in a second or third special work, we recognize that in practice we must yield more fully to God's grace and power in our lives.

The primary issue in Acts, however, is not subsequence or lack of subsequence. Although it was theologically normal to receive the full impact of the Spirit at conversion, whether people had the experience of empowerment was more important than when they received it. How many of us have yielded ourselves the way God wants us to, either at conversion or afterward, to the overwhelming direction of the Spirit in uttering praise, prophecy, or witness? That the apostles laid hands on the Samaritan Christians to make sure they "received the Spirit" shows that they regarded receiving the Spirit in this empowerment sense as normative, something Christians *must* have. Luke nowhere suggests that we need this work of the Spirit for salvation or spiritual virtue; it is a special empowerment for evangelism and the work of the kingdom. People differ over whether all Christians receive complete access to this power at their conversion (I believe they do) and debate what kind of manifestations may accompany the believer's experience of this empowerment. But aside from these issues, the fact remains that in practice we dare not miss Luke's point: we need the Spirit's power. If Luke wrote Acts to teach us anything in particular, then he expects the missionary church to be a Spirit-empowered church in experience, not just in theory.

Tongues-Speaking and Spirit Baptism

The assertion that tongues-speaking always accompanies baptism in the Spirit may represent the major, irreconcilable difference between traditional Pentecostals and those who disagree with them, as D. A. Carson notes:

> If the charismatic movement would firmly renounce, on biblical grounds, not the gift of tongues but the idea that tongues constitute a special sign of a second blessing, a very substantial part of the wall between charismatics and noncharismatics would come crashing down. Does 1 Corinthians 12 demand any less?[20]

Church groups today hold a variety of positions regarding tongues, from cessationism (the view that genuine tongues no longer occurs) to the view that tongues-speaking is mandatory for salvation (currently declining even among circles that officially hold the position). We will return to some of those views in chapter 2, but here we will address a critical question that often divides mainstream Pentecostals from other evangelicals: Does tongues-speaking always accompany Spirit baptism?

The controversy surrounding the relation of tongues to baptism in the Spirit, like the controversy over whether that baptism always occurs at conversion or may occur after it, has the potential to distract readers from the primary focus of the book. I initially wished to avoid the issue, but one editor persuaded me that this book should address it. Readers who fear that they may not be edified, however, are welcome to skip to the next chapter!

In the circles in which I move, most believers—including those of us who pray in tongues—regard tongues as simply one gift among many and as a useful resource for prayer (see the discussion of 1 Corinthians 14 in the next chapter). Committed Bible-believers in mainline denominations tend to stick together, so charismatics in those denominations tend to be like other evangelicals there.

Traditional Pentecostals and many charismatics, however, typically associate tongues with baptism in the Holy Spirit in Acts, and this position deserves a fairer evaluation than it often receives. Whether or not we wish to connect tongues with that experience, we cannot evade the fact that Acts at least sometimes, and probably often, makes the connection. The debate today is what we should *make of* that connection. It is important to air the differences, because many Pentecostals, charismatics, and noncharismatics often do not even know the reasons others give for their views.

Because we focus here on the evidence in Acts, I will concentrate on clarifying two positions: (1) the belief that tongues *always* accompanies baptism in the Spirit and (2) the belief that it is normal, but not mandatory, for tongues to accompany baptism in the Spirit. I will try to present both positions as fairly as I can.

My Experience with Tongues

Those who write about spiritual gifts should be honest about their background—whether charismatic, noncharismatic, or anticharismatic—since past experiences may shape how they approach the issue. My experience with tongues is so much a part of my Christian life that I must allow my readers to take it into account as they read how I address this issue.

Yet although I pray in tongues, my initial experience with tongues came entirely unexpectedly. I first heard the gospel on the way home from high school one day, and after arguing for forty-five minutes with the Baptists who shared it with me, I walked home trembling. Although I had been an atheist and found their arguments unconvincing, the Spirit was pressing me for a decision and would not stop pressing until I surrendered or told him to leave me. Within an hour I fell to my knees on my bedroom floor and asked God to save me. Instantly I felt something rushing through my body that I had never felt before, and I quickly jumped to my feet, wondering what was happening. I resolved to be a Christian henceforth, although I was not yet certain of all that this commitment entailed. On Sunday I went to a church, and a pastor prayed with me to accept Christ. Assured now that I had accepted Christ "properly," I felt the same overwhelming presence of God I had felt two days before and this time decided to yield to it fully.

In a moment I was so overwhelmed with the awesome majesty and presence of God that I understood that only he could provide me adequate words with which to praise him. And because I intuitively understood that God knows lots of languages, it somehow did not surprise me when the Spirit gave me another language in which to praise him. For an hour or two I worshiped God in tongues—often punctuated with deep, cathartic laughter (which has recurred on occasion since)—experiencing a joy I had never known before. When I finished, I was convinced that the purpose in life I had long sought must be to promote the glory of Jesus Christ alone.

Over the years God provided other experiences (including learning how to read the Bible in context) that made this spiritual experience only one among many, but prayer in tongues remains special to me in my personal prayer life. Having never read the Bible before that day or been exposed to speaking in tongues, I did not know "tongues" existed, nor did I hold preconceptions about what tongues should involve. But God simply granted me the gift as an act of grace to a former atheist who badly needed a touch from him.

I recognize that everyone's experience is different, but I offer my own story as an example of how God might provide an experience similar to the ones in Acts for a person who had not been taught anything pro or con about tongues. I also mention it so the reader may evaluate how my experience may have shaped my perspective in ways I am not aware. I only ask that each reader be equally honest about how his or her own experience or nonexperience may shape the way he or she approaches the biblical evidence. Because the circles in which we move may affect the way we approach issues, I should also acknowledge that many of the charismatics with whom I currently fellowship are Baptist and Methodist charismatics, for most of whom speaking in tongues is a "normal" (common) but not "normative" (mandatory) evidence of the Spirit's work. This differs somewhat from the traditional Pentecostal position, so traditional Pentecostals may wish to take into account whatever degree of influence this approach may exercise on my current thinking.

While tongues is not central in my theological reflection, it remains an integral part of my personal prayer experience, and I often see it repeated when I pray for new believers to experience the empowerment described above. In these times of prayer, the vast majority of people I pray with dramatically sense the overwhelming presence of God's Spirit, many in ways that they have never sensed before. Often (though not always) they begin to pray in tongues at that time; many others (though not all) end up doing so later (including some who insisted they never would!).

It should be able to go without saying that one need not be a traditional Pentecostal to pray in tongues. We Baptists, for instance, are supposed to have no "creed" but Scripture alone, and the gift is in Scripture. (My fellow Baptist Tony Campolo, on the other hand, has a nice book *How to Be Pentecostal without Speaking in Tongues*.[21] I guess that is the other side of it!) I am pleased with the growing consensus in much of the church: prayer in tongues is one useful way to pray, but not a valid way to determine how spiritual someone is. (If I could find the adjective in Scripture, I'd add that tongues is also "fun.") Prayer in tongues is spiritually helpful, but many of Christ's most devoted followers (including many of my dearest Christian friends) do not do it. Appreciating this broad area of common agreement, I intend not to challenge either Pentecostal or non-Pentecostal distinctives beyond this position, but rather to help those holding various positions to understand the other point of view.

I will therefore try my best to lay aside my own predispositions and objectively present the best evidence and views offered by both sides of the debate. It is easiest for me to speak about tongues from a noncontroversial Pauline perspective (praying with one's spirit); many noncharismatics are good Paulinists and find little offense in Paul's way of putting the matter. But the nature of this book requires me to be fair also to Luke's perspective in Acts, and I suspect that if Luke had been writing his book today, we might have called him a Pentecostal. Rather than arguing for only one position, I asked friends on various sides of the debate to read my presentation before this book was published, to make sure that it is fair to their side. I hope that both modern followers of Paul and of Luke can realize that since God inspired both writers, we should be open to the truth emphasized by movements built on the equally correct insights of either one. I believe that in practice these views are compatible—and Christians need not divide over their distinctive emphases. Not all theological issues lend themselves to such compatibility (for example, the Scriptures can hardly teach *both* a pre- and post-tribulation rapture), but more middle ground may exist on this issue.[22]

Tongues as the Evidence of Spirit Baptism?

Some texts appear to fit the traditional Pentecostal model better than many non-Pentecostals acknowledge. Although Luke's focus for baptism in the Spirit is evangelism rather than speaking in tongues (Acts 1:8), tongues clearly functions as the initial sign of baptism in the Spirit in Acts 2. In that chapter, the hearers who recognized the languages demanded, "What does *this* mean?" (2:12). Others in the audience charged the disciples with drunkenness (2:13). Peter responded to these comments in reverse (chiastic) order: the charge of drunkenness is manifestly absurd (2:15), but "this" is what Joel meant when he said the Spirit would be poured out and God's people would prophesy (2:16–18); hence the time of salvation has also come (2:19–21). Peter regarded tongues as the evidence that the Spirit had come, as evidence of the prophetic empowerment promised by Joel. Acts 2 becomes a paradigm, or model, for the Spirit-empowerment of the church in Acts.

Moreover, tongues-speaking fulfills the same function in Acts 10:46–47 ("they received the Spirit the same way we did") and accompanies prophecy in fulfilling the role of evidencing prophetic empowerment in Acts 19:6. Tongues-speaking is not mentioned at the initial reception of the Spirit among the Samaritan converts in Acts 8 and by Paul in Acts 9. However, *something* tangible happened in Acts 8 (Simon saw and wanted it), and 1 Corinthians 14:18 indicates that Paul at some point began speaking in tongues. Because the narrative in Acts 9 predicts (but does not describe) Paul's reception of the Spirit, one cannot conclude from Luke's silence that tongues-speaking did not occur on that occasion. One may only conclude that whether or not it occurred, Luke did not seek to emphasize it at that point. Some Pentecostal scholars have argued that tongues accompanies baptism in the Holy Spirit the way water baptism accompanies conversion: Luke does not mention baptism after every conversion, but he expects the reader to infer it from the cases in which it is stated. Perhaps the experience of tongues was so typical in Luke's circle of Christianity that readers simply assumed that tongues accompanied baptism in the Spirit, even when tongues was not mentioned.

Traditional Pentecostals find in such narrative data confirmation of their belief that speaking in tongues provides the initial physical evidence of Spirit baptism. According to one version of early Pentecostal history, Charles Parham in December 1900 instructed his students to inductively and independently determine the evidence of baptism in the Spirit in Acts. When all the students independently arrived at the conclusion that tongues evidenced Spirit baptism, the group decided to pray for the gift. God initiated a revival movement, especially launched under William Seymour's direction at Azusa Street, that now counts over 350 million Pentecostals and charismatics around the world. Seymour himself was so convinced that speaking in tongues was biblical that he began preaching it months before he had experienced it himself.

Most traditional North American Pentecostals argue that tongues-speaking always accompanies Spirit baptism. Yet some Pentecostals disagree (especially many in places like Chile and Germany), as do a significant percentage of nondenominational and mainline charismatics, including the growing Vineyard movement. Given the evidence above, many of those who believe that the gifts of the Spirit continue today concede that tongues often accompanied Spirit baptism in Acts and fail to be surprised when the two occur together today. For reasons supplied in our appendix, "What Can Bible Stories Teach Us?" many will concede that Acts provides us models for the Spirit-filled church (especially where the Spirit himself acts directly), not solely a description of an early stage of the church.

But despite these concessions, noncharismatics, many charismatics, and some Pentecostals today point out that Luke's using narrative to teach does not automatically guarantee consensus on *what* Luke wished to teach. Thus British New Testament scholar James D. G. Dunn traces the initial reception of the Spirit through Acts and concludes that in every instance where receiving the Spirit is described, Christians seem to have spoken in tongues. Thus "the corollary is then not without force that Luke *intended* to portray 'speaking in tongues' as 'the initial physical evidence' of the outpouring of the Spirit." But Dunn goes on to note that while Luke focuses on such tangible evidences of the Spirit's presence, he clearly also includes praise (10:45–46), prophecy (19:6), and boldness (4:8, 31); and if Luke wished to emphasize tongues as the *necessary* evidence, he would have mentioned it more explicitly in Acts 8.[23]

Those who believe in tongues, but who doubt that it always accompanies baptism in the Spirit, thus can raise important objections to the view that tongues invariably accompanies baptism in the Holy Spirit. Because tongues is a form of inspired speech, Luke could often use it to inform readers that people in his narrative had received prophetic empowerment. Saying that genuine manifestations of tongues guarantee that prophetic empowerment has come need not, however, imply that prophetic empowerment always is accompanied by tongues. That is, because genuine tongues-speakers are baptized in the Spirit, this need not imply that all Spirit-baptized people must speak in tongues. (In the same way, one might reason that all true apostles are Christians, but not all true Christians are apostles.)

Luke's intention, as well as we can infer it from his text, is to demonstrate that the outpouring of the Spirit on Pentecost continues to mark the advance of Christianity to all peoples. Each stage in the expansion of the gospel in Acts is marked by prophetic empowerment empirically demonstrated, as in the Church's first experience, with tongues. That is, Luke is teaching us about the Spirit by means of the evidence of tongues, rather than about tongues by examples of people receiving the Spirit. He may prefer to emphasize tongues as a sign because it symbolically reinforces his theme of cross-cultural witness (Acts 1:8). Most readers note that, whatever one might wish to infer happened in the cases in Acts where tongues are not explicitly mentioned, that Luke did not mention their occurrence suggests that he is not intentionally teaching that tongues always accompanies Spirit baptism. And if he is not teaching it, they note, we lack a single New Testament passage that explicitly teaches that doctrine.

Classical Pentecostals may respond, however, that this caveat does not settle the case against tongues accompanying the baptism in the Spirit. Some have argued that even if the Book of Acts does not *explicitly* teach this doctrine, it may nevertheless serve as a window into early Christian experience. At the very least, Acts indicates a pattern in which tongues often accompanied the experience it describes. Given the brevity and narrow focus of Acts, surely the Spirit worked in many ways for which little clear record remains. Many important early Christian doctrines appear in the New Testament writings only because controversy surrounded them (for example, the Lord's Supper in 1 Cor. 11:17–34). The New Testament is not a doctrine manual written by a symposium of theologians, but a collection of essential inspired writings from the earliest Christians commissioned by our Lord. Thus, claiming that no texts in the Bible conclusively *prove* the Pentecostal position is not the same as saying that this *disproves* the Pentecostal position. The usual classical Pentecostal view that tongues-speaking necessarily and immediately accompanies baptism in the Holy Spirit could still be true, attested by some other means such as Pentecostal experience. Further, the close connection in Acts between tongues and the baptism in the Spirit would have made the most sense to an audience where the two frequently occurred together.

Non-Pentecostals will, however, also respond to this Pentecostal objection. If early Christians would not acknowledge that baptism in the Spirit had occurred unless the person began speaking in tongues, it is surprising that the rest of the New Testament does not preserve more testimonies to such a central evidence. Further, it is questionable whether even modern Pentecostal experience proves that tongues must always accompany baptism in the Spirit, at least immediately (unless one argues circularly that a powerful charismatic experience is not genuine Spirit baptism without tongues). (The Pentecostal argument from Scripture at this point is stronger than their argument from experience.) Some charismatics consider it presumptuous to insist that tongues accompany baptism in the Spirit, as presumptuous as declaring that God heals without exception if we have enough faith.

Further, one may argue, most Pentecostals do not hold God to every other pattern in Scripture. Although in both Acts and 1 Corinthians tongues seem to be used only in prayer (see discussion of this point in the next chapter), many Pentecostals justify a "message in tongues" by insisting that God can do whatever he wants. Yet if the biblical pattern does not hold in all situations (God can, after all, do anything that does not contradict his nature), must God *always* confer tongues when baptizing his children in his Spirit? For instance, would God withhold the empowerment of his Spirit from those who had been taught to fear tongues and wait until they had overcome their fear? Most of us who move in noncharismatic circles have many Christian friends who live deeply Spirit-led lives without tongues, some of whom act more empowered for holiness and witness than many who speak in tongues. Tongues might bless their prayer life, but they already have some greater gifts to offer the rest of Christ's body.

Noncharismatics also point to Paul's claim that not all speak in tongues (1 Cor. 12:30). In the context, Paul is arguing that although we need all the gifts in the body of Christ, one should not regard one's own gifts as superior or inferior to the others. Pentecostals usually respond to this argument in one of two ways. First, Pentecostals traditionally argue that Paul here refers to the public gift of tongues rather than to private prayer language (a distinction which the context may support, but which may also have more to do with the way the gift is being used than with an intrinsic difference between the two forms of tongues themselves). Second, some Pentecostals also cite 1 Corinthians 14:5 to suggest that even if not all Christians speak in tongues, Paul thinks that it would be a good idea for them to do so. Whether one interprets 14:5 in light of 1 Corinthians 12:30 or the reverse, however, often depends on the view one starts with. The debaters may stalemate on this point, unable to win much ground from the other side.

Some charismatics have pointed out that the traditional Pentecostal position is not completely monolithic; some classical Pentecostals rejected it. Agnes Ozman (the first person to speak in tongues at the beginning of the modern Pentecostal revival), F. F. Bosworth, and other prominent early Pentecostals questioned whether tongues always accompanied Spirit baptism.[24] Indeed, even today it is mostly a shared experience rather than a common way of formulating that experience that connects charismatics in Pentecostal and various independent and mainline churches.

Perhaps most significantly, William Seymour, leader of the Azusa Street Revival, denied that tongues was "*the* evidence" of the baptism in the Holy Spirit. Seymour had originally accepted Charles Parham's teaching that tongues represented the initial sign of Spirit baptism, but when confronted with Parham's own behavior—reportedly including his White racist rhetoric directed against Seymour, who was Black—Seymour came to question whether Parham was even saved, since he lacked the fruit of the Spirit in his life. Although Seymour continued to affirm the importance of tongues-speaking, he rejected the doctrine that tongues must always accompany Spirit baptism. Considering it a false doctrine that bound God, he regarded it as a form of idolatry.[25]

Others have also stressed that the Spirit's fruit is a clearer sign of the Spirit's work than tongues. Wesley accepted revelations, prophecies, healings, and so forth among his followers, but he emphasized that the true evidence of the Spirit was maturation toward Christian perfection. Some early Pentecostals also stressed love as the primary evidence. For instance, Pandita Ramabai, the leading figure in the early-twentieth-century outpouring of the Spirit in India, stressed that while tongues was one sign of baptism in the Spirit, the essential and inevitable sign was love.[26] Classical Pentecostals usually respond that the Spirit's fruit is an essential sign of his presence, but tongues-speaking is (as noted above) the most frequent mark of the initial experience depicted in Acts, a pattern most Pentecostals believe is normative.

Depending on which side of the discussion bears the burden of proof, that is about where the biblical evidence in the debate between many Pentecostals and non-Pentecostals ends: Acts shows that tongues often accompanies one's first filling with prophetic empowerment, but Acts by itself is hard-pressed to prove that it always must do so. Although most non-Pentecostals therefore remain skeptical about whether we can conclude that someone is not filled (even in the Acts sense) because he or she has not spoken in tongues, those sensitive to the text should at least appreciate traditional Pentecostal exegetes for bringing to our attention an inescapable feature of the Acts narratives: in Acts, tongues frequently accompanies being filled with the Spirit for the first time, sometimes in conjunction with other Spirit-anointed speech like prophecy. Although Christians continue to dispute whether tongues occurs in every instance in Acts (and even more so whether it must regularly occur today), Luke uses tongues far more than any other sign to indicate that believers have received the Spirit's prophetic empowerment. By pointing to tongues, Pentecostals have reminded us that being filled with the Spirit in the Lukan sense is empowerment to speak God's message (Acts 1:8), an ability to speak with special sensitivity what the Spirit puts in our hearts (Acts 4:31; compare Eph. 5:18–20).

Whether by praying in tongues or by other means, all of us can profit by inculcating deeper sensitivity to the Spirit's leading in our words. Some charismatics, including myself, have found that spiritual sensitivity developed during prayer in a lan-

guage we do not know has helped us pray and witness more effectively in the languages that we do know. But on any view, prayer
and witness is more central biblically than whether we offer it
in an unknown language. We will raise additional questions about
tongues at appropriate points in chapter 2.

Considering the Practical Issues

Entirely aside from the above questions, both charismatics
and noncharismatics agree that our spiritual quest should emphasize the Spirit, not tongues—a matter that some have been
known to forget in practice. And when we ask God to empower
us to pray in tongues, should we be asking him for "evidence"
that we have had a spiritual experience or for a fresh way to pray
and worship him? Even if one believes that tongues evidenced
Spirit-reception in Acts (and in at least three cases they do serve
that literary function), Acts provides no indication that Christians should seek them for this purpose. I recall friends who went
on long fasts, experienced visions, or witnessed boldly, but who
later rejected the Christian faith. This observation does not
demean fasting, visions, or witness, but suggests appropriate priorities. Ultimately, any focus—no matter how good in itself—
that replaces allegiance to Christ himself will become a counterfeit. Tongues, like every other gift, functions best when Christ
rather than the gift summons our attention.

This book will not be able to reconcile two positions on
tongues and the baptism in the Spirit that differ as much as do
the classical Pentecostal and noncharismatic positions, but I
emphasize again that, despite this difference, both sides have
more common ground *on the most important issues* than differences. Biblically we should acknowledge that tongues often
accompany a spiritual experience described in the Book of
Acts. We can also agree that what is most important about the
experience is not tongues-speaking itself, but empowerment
for mission. And in practice, the argument may be less about

initial evidence than about other important concerns. One of the standard pragmatic reasons for traditional Pentecostal insistence on maintaining the "initial evidence" doctrine is the concern that Pentecostals will stop seeking the ability to pray in tongues if the doctrine is abandoned.

As long as traditional Pentecostals and charismatics are the primary people seeking the gift, many will probably continue to feel the pressure to make sure as many as possible of their number function in that gift. Yet if (as we suggest in the next chapter on spiritual gifts) tongues is a useful gift for private prayer and one may approach God in prayer for spiritual gifts, "necessary evidence of Spirit baptism" is not the only reason for seeking the gift.[27] Praying in tongues, like other forms of prayer, can add a new dimension to one's prayer life. Few of us would claim to be proficient in all forms of prayer, and most of us, charismatic or noncharismatic, desire more help from the Spirit when we pray. This approach also makes immediate results seem less urgent, avoids the temptation to grade people spiritually on the basis of whether or not they speak in tongues, and prevents despair among those who have long sought for the gift and not received it.[28]

Because most Christians today are not *against* speaking in tongues, as was the case in an earlier era, it may be less important for Pentecostals to focus as much attention on defending the doctrine as previously. Many Christians seem ready to move beyond the controversy over tongues and begin to explore all that God's Spirit has for us (often including, but not limited to, prayer in tongues). Most of us will agree that in the whole biblical perspective on the Spirit, we should focus on the Spirit's provision of an intimate relationship with our risen Lord Jesus and empowerment to make him known and to live out the fruit of the Spirit. We need the Spirit to transform our hearts to imitate Christ's character and to persevere through testings.

If we think ourselves filled with God's Spirit because we speak in tongues, yet neglect his call to evangelize the world, to stand for justice for the oppressed and for the righteousness of God's Word, we deceive ourselves. True charismatics must live their whole lives in the power of God's Spirit. If all North American Christians began speaking in tongues tomorrow, that would not constitute revival. But if all North American Christians began loving Jesus and one another passionately enough to fulfill the Great Commission, we would experience a revival like the world has never before seen.

When in doubt, most Christians fall back on denominational views for the details, hopefully without disrespecting Christian brothers and sisters in different denominations. Beyond more easily disputed issues, however, I believe that some practical issues are clear from the New Testament witness: (1) speaking in tongues is a very natural manifestation of the Spirit's presence in Spirit baptism (the way Luke means it); (2) tongues constitute a valid form of worship to God (see chapter 2); (3) the purpose for desiring this gift should be the worship of God rather than even the slightest hint of spiritual elitism; and (4) tongues used for private worship can strengthen one's prayer life. If some Christians have overemphasized tongues in response to others who have played it down, they have at least called us back to a biblical appreciation of the gift and to a hunger for deeper intimacy with God.

Conclusion

We are complete in Christ and dead to sin, but that neither means that all of us always live accordingly nor that we always appropriate the power of the Spirit that enables us to do so. Conversion gives us access to all we need, but neither conversion nor a single experience after conversion frees us from the need to seek God's empowerment in practice. We seek not a single *experience*, but a continuing *relationship*, daily encountering our master in the power of his Holy Spirit, living out of the power already imparted to us when we became followers of Jesus Christ. Both noncharismatic and charismatic Christians can use more of the Spirit's power in their daily walk of obedient faith in God. I would not dare to face my calling and the conflicts my calling entails without the Spirit, and I think that I am not alone. Aren't there many of us who could use a deeper sensitivity to God's Spirit, whether in crisis experiences at needed moments or in the gentle flow of his Spirit within us each day?

Variously gifted parts of Christ's body can help one another by sharing their gifts rather than by negating others' gifts, whether the gift be tongues or wisdom and knowledge. Noncharismatics can learn much from the experiences of charismatics. Similarly, we can learn more about how to read the Bible from those who are strongest in exegetical skills, about God's concern for the broken and wounded from those who have learned to share others' pain, and so on. We are one body, and we need one another's gifts. If Satan's kingdom cannot stand if divided, we must also question whether the church serves Christ best by dividing from one another. We are members of one another and should bring all our gifts together to build up his one body (Rom. 12:4–8; 1 Cor. 12:7).

What is the baptism in the Holy Spirit? Aside from debates about how much of God's empowerment occurs at what point in the believer's life, the baptism in the Holy Spirit is God's empowerment for the mission he has given the church. God has made us new by his Spirit and now enables us to live new lives and build up our worshiping communities by the Spirit's fruit and gifts (Paul). God has washed us, causing us to be born from him with a new character (John). Through the empowerment of God's Spirit, we are called to take Jesus' message both to those around us and to the ends of the earth (Acts).

Through the empowerment of God's Spirit, Jesus prepares us to face the conflicts of our mission, confronting and defeating the devil at the point of human need (Mark). The Spirit transforms us when we come to Christ; from that point forward we should continue to depend on his power to carry out the mission Jesus gave us.

How Important Are Spiritual Gifts Today?

had volunteered to do the class presentation on Bultmann in our Ph.D. seminar on biblical interpretation. After summarizing some of Bultmann's positive contributions to biblical scholarship, I critiqued what I thought was a fatal flaw in his rejection of biblical miracles: "Bultmann declares that no one in the modern world believes in miracles—and thereby excludes most people today from the modern world."

I had scanned the classroom before speaking, silently counting the number of students who would likely agree that God has done miracles. "His belief that modern people cannot accept God acting visibly in history excludes from the modern world most of us around this table," I continued. "Indeed, Bultmann excludes not only orthodox Christians, Jews, and Muslims, but spiritists, traditional tribal religionists, and others who believe in supernatural phenomena—in short, everyone but Western rationalists and atheistic Marxists. Bultmann defines the modern world simply on the basis of his mid-twentieth-century Western academic elitism—making him an ethnocentric cultural bigot."

Naturally, my professor, whom we knew to be the school's last remaining Bultmannian, objected. "Bultmann has his presuppositions, but you have your presuppositions, too!" he responded, more than mildly irritated.

"That is true," I conceded. "When I was an atheist, I denied that miracles could happen. As a Christian, I insist that God can do miracles. But an agnostic, neutral starting point would be to ask: What evidence is there for or against miracles? To argue against miracles inductively, Bultmann would have to examine every possible claim to a miracle and show it to be false (and even then he would not have proved that such a claim could *never* be true). But all I have to do to begin to argue that miracles *do* happen is to cite credible eyewitness evidence." So I started doing just that—listing instantaneous healings I had witnessed in answer to believing prayers, particularly when I had been the person healed or the person praying for another's healing. Finally I concluded, "Now if anyone still wishes to deny that miracles can happen, the next logical step is to challenge my credibility as a reliable eyewitness." The professor quickly changed the subject.

Yet Bultmannian professors are hardly alone in their skepticism. After the rise of the modern Western prejudice against miracles, some Christians, while acknowledging that miracles happened in the Bible, created a system that forced them to discount evidence that miracles happen in modern times. Their skepticism is perhaps understandable. This is not the first time in history that circumstances led God's people to wonder whether God could continue his powerful works in their generation (Judg. 6:13). Many other Christians who acknowledge that God can still do miracles in answer to prayer claim that supernatural gifts have ceased, thus doubting that God does miracles the same way he did them in biblical times.[1] Probably the majority of Christians today acknowledge that supernatural gifts remain available, although few of us currently witness them with the same magnitude and regularity as in Acts.

Yet many of us who acknowledge that miracles can happen today (including some Pentecostals) would be scared out of our wits if one actually happened to us. So pervasively has Enlightenment culture's antisupernaturalism affected the Western church, especially educated White European and North American Christians, that most of us are suspicious of anything supernatural. Is it possible that God has something more to teach his church today about supernatural gifts?

The Controversy

Spiritual gifts have become a major issue of controversy in our generation, especially since the charismatic revival has taken the experience of these gifts beyond the confines of mainline Pentecostalism. Some observers continue to maintain what is called the traditional "cessationist" position: supernatural spiritual gifts—that is, any that we cannot also explain in natural terms—have passed away. Proponents of this position usually argue it from 1 Corinthians 13:8–10 or Ephesians 2:20 and especially from history. But the evidence for their interpretation of these texts and of history is hotly and rightly disputed by others.[2] These observers must then find other explanations for charismatic phenomena among genuine fellow Christians. In the past some attributed them to demons, but psychological explanations are more frequent today.

The argument that spiritual gifts ceased in history, however, would not be a very good argument against spiritual gifts today even if it were certainly true. That gifts *should* cease is not a logical conclusion from the assertion that they *did* cease. First, signs and wonders waxed and waned from one period to another (though they were never absent) even in the Bible; they especially spread in times of revival. Second, the argument that gifts did cease and therefore should cease is an argument based on one kind of experience. Yet those who make this argument simply dismiss the experience of hundreds of millions of Christians today (estimated at over 350 million—Pentecostals and charismatics may represent the largest single block of Christians after Roman Catholicism). Some claimed spiritual experiences are inauthentic, but cessationists must be quite sure of their exegesis before they dismiss *all* of them. Yet I think it no coincidence that cessationism arose only in a culture dominated by anti-supernaturalism.[3]

Other observers, while acknowledging that these gifts could in *theory* occur today, have been understandably reticent to embrace them because of the excesses that have occurred in charismatic circles in recent decades. Other contemporary positions exist as well. Some approve of spiritual gifts in principle, but have had little contact with them personally and find little reason to actively seek them for their own lives. Others embrace spiritual gifts personally, but feel that other issues in the church take precedence. Still others (probably representing the majority of mainline Pentecostals and charismatics) believe that spiritual gifts are critical and that the whole church should embrace them. Finally, a minority of people (mainly in traditional United Pentecostal and some Apostolic circles) believe that the particular gift of tongues-speaking is essential for salvation. (Yet I know a number of people even in those churches who do *not* hold this view.) From my own and others' observations of various sectors of the body of Christ, it appears that both extremes—the extreme cessationists (who deny miraculous gifts today) and those who require tongues for salvation—are becoming an increasingly small minority. Most Christians fall into various moderate positions between these two extremes.

Like other recent charismatic scholars such as Gordon Fee and former cessationist Jack Deere, I believe that the position that supernatural gifts have ceased is one that no Bible reader would hold if not previously taught to do so. At the same time, I would contend that the other extreme is far more serious: adding any condition to salvation—whether tongues-speaking or anything else—distorts the sufficiency of Christ and enters the realm of *heresy*. Many people who hold some dangerous views in theory are fortunately not consistent with those views in practice, and undoubtedly many who claim to hold this view in theory are our brothers and sisters in Christ. But however Christian in practice some holders of the tongues-for-salvation view may be, the view itself is still a deadly distortion of Christ's gospel.

The mediating views not only fall within mainstream evangelicalism but differ on relatively minor points. Many of us hold a somewhat eclectic position, which may emerge as the general consensus (if a consensus emerges). We do not believe that supernatural gifts represent the most important issue facing the church today, but we do believe that they point us to a more crucial issue: they call us to dependence on God's Spirit in our ministry to others. We do not believe that those who exercise particular spiritual gifts are more "spiritual" than others, but we affirm that all spiritual gifts should rightly belong to the whole body of Christ today (rather than specific gifts being segregated into specific parts of the church). God provides gifts to serve the church, not to exalt individuals as the Corinthians did. Many of us believe from experience that there are nondivisive ways to teach noncharismatic churches about spiritual gifts from the Bible (especially by not overemphasizing them to the exclusion of other critical issues) that can sensitize them to greater dependence on the Spirit. Many Pentecostal churches will likewise profit from a fresh examination of spiritual gifts, because among Pentecostals, as among non-Pentecostals, many of the gifts rarely function adequately.

I should add at this point that I am using "charismatic" in a broad sense in this context, applying the term to those who embrace spiritual gifts in practice rather than to views held in some circles within the charismatic movement. In the broadest sense, of course, all Christians are charismatic, because God "gifted" each of us with a special role and purpose when the Spirit baptized us into Christ's body (1 Cor. 12:7–13; *charisma* means "grace-gift"). But even when one applies the label more narrowly to those who insist that all churches should be open to all spiritual gifts, the term does not connote every view held by some charismatics. Many noncharismatics rightly object to questionable teachings held by many charismatics (for example, "prosperity" teaching) and to the way a number of popular charismatic ministers handle Scripture (frequently without giving attention to context). (Regardless of who gets the most coverage on some television programs, most biblically literate mainstream charismatics I know reject prosperity teaching, "revelations" that take Scripture out of context, and so forth.) Yet these practices have nothing to do with being charismatic per se—that is, they have nothing to do with charismatic views concerning spiritual gifts. In fact, many anticharismatic fundamentalist ministers have applied Scripture with equal disregard for its context, and many who disavow prosperity teaching are not for that reason any less materialistic.

Further, while such teachings do call into question how sensitively those charismatics are functioning in the spiritual gift of *teaching*, they need not in every case negate the reality of their personal experience in the Holy Spirit. Teaching is admittedly one of the higher-ranking gifts (1 Cor. 12:28), and those whose teaching is unsound disqualify themselves from the office of pastor (1 Tim. 3:2; 2 Tim. 2:24; Titus 1:9). Nevertheless, to teach soundly we teachers must acknowledge the need for other gifts as well. As diverse members of Christ's body we all need one another and need to draw on one another's gifts (1 Cor. 12:28–31). That one person lacks the gift of teaching and another, say, gifts of healings, is all the more reason to begin to learn from one another's gifts. When we yield to God's Spirit, he brings forth the fruit of humility so we can learn from one another (Gal. 5:22–6:2), maintaining the unity of the Spirit in Christ's body (Eph. 4:3–13). Then we are more likely to gain a hearing when we seek to bring greater truth to the rest of the church.

We will examine several lines of evidence suggesting that miracles and supernatural gifts should continue to function in today's church. Although many other lines of evidence are possible, we seek here to provide merely a sample of the arguments that could be offered.[4] *First,* the Gospel writers (in this case we will use Matthew as an example) present Jesus' miracle-working ministry as a model for disciples. (This does not, of course, imply that all of us will be equally proficient in all gifts, as Paul points out.) *Second,* Luke presents the empowerment of the church at Pentecost as a normative experience for Christians. As we noted above, this experience includes empowerment to speak by the Spirit's inspiration, especially for witness, and in Acts at least often includes inspired utterances like prophecy or tongues. *Third,* Paul's presentation of the gifts is inseparable from his view of the church. That is, Paul believes that every member of Christ's body has a special function for his or her gift. Paul does not envision any of these specific functions in the body ceasing to be operative before the Lord's return; indeed, he explicitly declares that our imperfect gifts will cease at that time (1 Cor. 13:8–13).

Are Miraculous Signs of the Kingdom for Today? (Matthew)

As noted above, Mark portrays Jesus as the one who can answer his people's prayers, and emphasizes that Jesus empowers his followers both to do miracles and to suffer for his honor. Matthew recounts this same point from another perspective. In chapters 8 and 9, Matthew provides ten specific examples of Jesus' healing power in nine accounts, interweaving these practical demonstrations of Jesus' authority with a recurring summons to submit to that authority (8:18–22; 9:9–17, 35–38). Although the Gospel writers draw spiritual points from these accounts, most of these stories teach us something about physical healing as well.

Let us take the example of the cleansing of the leper in Matthew 8:1–4. It is important to note that the leper approaches Jesus with complete trust in his authority. He likewise humbly acknowledges that the choice of whether or not he is healed belongs to Jesus (8:2). Acknowledging that God has the right to refuse a specific prayer need not indicate a lack of faith, as some suppose. It may simply indicate respect for God's authority (Gen. 18:27, 30, 32). Biblical faith is not a formula by which God can be manipulated, but a relationship with one whose character we have come to trust. At the same time, Matthew shows us something about Jesus' character: he *wanted* to heal the man (8:3; Mark 1:41 speaks of Jesus' "compassion"). Jesus was so concerned with the man's condition that he touched the untouchable, thereby sharing the leper's uncleanness in the eyes of his own culture (8:3). Whatever God's purposes may be in a specific situation, none of us would doubt that Jesus' character and compassion remain the same today.

Another healing story includes two miracles: the healing of a woman who had been bleeding for years and the raising of a dead girl. Jesus again appeared ready to heal and even to restore to life (9:18–19). The bleeding woman adds a new element of teaching to the story, however. She had *scandalous* faith (9:20–21). Under biblical and Jewish law, this woman communicated ritual impurity to anyone she touched; so for her to press her way to Jesus in a crowd was scandalous. For her to intentionally touch Jesus' cloak—thereby rendering him unclean in the eyes of observant Jews—was even more scandalous. Yet she was desperate. She lived in a society where women could not earn adequate money to survive on their own, and her condition virtually guaranteed that she could never marry. So convinced was she of Jesus' power, that she acted scandalously, desperately staking everything on his ability to heal her. The narrative concludes, not with Jesus rejecting her or concealing her touch, but with his publicly acknowledging her condition and sharing her uncleanness in the eyes of society so that he could publicly pronounce her healed (9:22). Jesus accepted her desperation as an act of faith (9:22). That our Lord Jesus is like this should not surprise us: he is the one who bore our infirmities, suffering in our place so we might go free (8:17).

Matthew emphasizes that compassion was Jesus' primary motivation for ministry to people (9:36). If his character remains the same today, we may be confident that Jesus still wishes to heal and deliver many people as he did long ago. But Jesus also explicitly declares that he needs more workers to complete the task of proclaiming the kingdom and healing (9:37–38). When Jesus came in the flesh, he could be in only one place at a time; hence he was limited in how much he could do until he trained others to help with the work (9:37). So he instructed his disciples to pray for more workers (9:38). One need not read much further to find that those Jesus taught to share his compassion in prayer became workers themselves (Matthew 10). Thus Jesus multiplied his mission by means of his followers.

Some aspects of this first mission, like limiting it to Israel (10:5–6), are later specifically revoked (28:19). But for the most part, Matthew intends the mission discourse in chapter 10 as a model to teach the church how to continue to evangelize. This is clear because

1. The commission to "go" makes this passage a model for the Great Commission in 28:19 (although the empha-

sis there is on disciple-making through baptizing and instructing).

2. The disciples here perpetuate the kingdom message of John the Baptist and Jesus (3:2; 4:17; 9:35; 10:7), and this message of God's authority is also ours today (28:18–19).

3. The disciples are to *demonstrate* God's reign the way Jesus did, through healings and exorcisms (9:35; 10:8), a commission Matthew nowhere revokes (in contrast to his subsequent revoking of 10:5–6).

4. These signs fulfill Scripture and attest not simply to Jesus' earthly ministry but also to his message of the new era, the kingdom of God (11:4–6; see Isa. 35:5–6).

5. The compassion that motivated Jesus (9:36) remains operative, as does the principle of agency for those who remain Christ's representatives by the gospel (10:40–42).

6. Acts and Paul's writings show us that Jesus' commission to heal and to live simply remained the standard for early Christian missionaries.

7. Most tellingly, Matthew here includes material about the end time that comes from elsewhere in Mark. (Ancient biographers had the freedom to rearrange their sources.) Like Mark, whom we examined in chapter 1, Matthew believes that Spirit-empowered ministry involves persecution (10:17–39).

Especially in view of point 7, Matthew does not just tell us about the first disciples' commission (though he does that too); he also tells us that this mission must continue and will not be completed until the Son of Man returns (10:23). Thus Matthew intends this discourse as missionary instructions for his own audience, not just a rehearsal of the past. Each of the above points could be defended in greater detail, but together they suggest that the signs of the kingdom should continue among us today. By systematically excluding enough of the biblical evidence from consideration (say, all narrative or, worse yet, all biblical evidence before the death of the apostles), one can prove almost anything. But if the whole New Testament speaks to us, what John Wimber and others call "power evangelism" should remain one important method of evangelism.

Is the Gift of Pentecost for Today? (Acts)

Although we addressed Pentecost in chapter 1, we need to add some observations here concerning the continuance of the gift of Pentecost. Referring to the "gift of the Spirit" earlier promised to all believers (Acts 1:4–5), Peter explicitly says that "this promise" is not only for all his hearers who turn to Christ, but for their descendants and "all who are far off," all whom the Lord calls (2:38–39). Perhaps unwittingly at this point, Peter speaks the language of Scripture: those who are "far off" represent the rest of Joel's "all flesh," the Gentiles (Eph. 2:17; Isa. 57:19). Peter had also quoted, "Whoever calls on the name of the Lord shall be saved," from Joel 2:32 (Acts 2:21). He spent the rest of his sermon explaining that this invitation refers to calling specifically on the name of Jesus (Acts 2:25, 34–36). Now he finishes the line from Joel 2:32: "all that the Lord calls" (Acts 2:39). The gift of the Spirit rightly belongs to all who turn from sin and accept Jesus Christ as Lord. Acts assumes that the gift made available at Pentecost remains in force.

Further, Peter's opening quote from Joel indicates that the gift *must* remain today. Peter correctly interprets Joel's prophecy as referring to "the last days" (2:17), understanding from Joel's context and from that of other prophets (for example, Isa. 44:3) that God would pour out his Spirit in the end time. "Last days" was a biblical expression for that period (Isa. 2:2; Micah 4:1). The outpoured Spirit signals that Christ has taken his seat at the Father's right hand (Acts 2:33–35; Ps. 110:1), and that his reign has in one sense been inaugurated. Unless God allowed the last days to begin and then retracted them—pouring out his Spirit and then pouring his Spirit back, attesting Christ's reign and then concealing it—we must still be in the era of the outpoured Spirit.

More to the point, the very structure of Peter's argument requires that this gift be available throughout this present age as people are saved through trusting in Christ. When foreigners are amazed to hear disciples speaking in other languages under the Spirit's inspiration, Peter insists that this fulfills Joel's prophecy about the Spirit of prophecy being poured out in the last days. This being the case, Peter argues, the rest of the prophecy is also in effect: whoever calls on the name of the Lord will be saved (2:21). Salvation and the gift of the Spirit belong to the same era; indeed, those who embrace Jesus receive the gift at conversion (2:38; see the discussion above in chapter 1).

Not all aspects of Pentecost are normative. Some aspects of the first Pentecost—like the wind and fire—were not repeated after Acts 2. But while some narratives in Acts do leave room for debate as to how frequently tongues accompanied the gift of the Spirit, in practice tongues (alongside prophecy) clearly marked reception of the Spirit's prophetic empowerment (ability to speak for God) in Acts 2:4, 10:44–47, and 19:6. In fact, when Peter hears the Gentiles speaking in tongues, he marvels that they "received the Spirit in the very same way that we did" (10:47). Since (1) the gift is permanent (2:39), (2) Luke three times uses tongues-speaking to attest the reception of the gift, (3) he depicts this response as a phenomenon arising from the Spirit's inspiration rather than from human culture (2:4), and finally, (4) he nowhere implies that this phenomenon was to cease, a heavy burden of proof lies on anyone who would argue that tongues have ceased today. Luke presents a model of the Spirit's working in his narratives, and if he had wished to restrict aspects of the model that were not relevant to his audience, we would expect him to have made this restriction clear.

Likewise, one who would argue that the "other" tongues merely represent the disciples' own languages (Greek and Aramaic) likewise unreasonably stretches the sense of the text to support one's thesis. Aramaic and Greek were hardly "other" tongues—both Greek-speaking and some Aramaic-speaking foreign Jews (who are Luke's primary focus in the text) and all the more so local Jews were conversant with these languages. No ancient texts suggest that local languages in Palestine could have been viewed as "other" tongues. Explaining away the supernatural empowerment to speak in languages the disciples had not learned requires ignoring both details of the text and features of the culture, no matter how well one may argue some individual points that contribute to this thesis.

Nor is the continuing work of the Spirit in Acts limited to speaking in tongues. Acts emphasizes the miracle-working ministries practiced by the original apostles (5:12), later apostles (14:3), and other Spirit-empowered witnesses (6:8). In Acts, signs and wonders remain the primary method of drawing people's attention to the gospel (see 2:5–41, 43; 3:11–4:4; 5:10–11, 12–16; 6:3, 5, 8–10; 8:6–7, 13, 39–40; 9:34–35, 40–42; 13:9–12; 15:12; 16:25–34; 19:11–20; 28:5–6, 8–10;[5] see especially 4:29–31; 14:3, 9), although well-educated Christians also engaged in public lecture and debate forums (6:8–10; 17:2–3; 18:28; 19:8–10), and the gospel was also passed on through the personal witness of individual Christians (8:4).

The Spirit's supernatural empowerment for our witness is a critical feature in Acts. Eyewitness testimony of what one has "heard and seen" applies both to eyewitnesses of the risen Christ (4:20) and to eyewitnesses of subsequent phenomena performed by his power (2:33; compare Luke 2:20). Moreover, the "word of God" or "word of the Lord," which in the Old Testament referred primarily to the past or present proclamation of God's prophets, in Acts refers especially to the saving gospel of Christ (6:7; 8:4, 14; 10:44; 13:44; 14:3; 16:32; 17:13; 19:20). Whether through the Spirit's leading in our words, or by God sometimes answering our prayers in ways that demonstrate the reality of his reign, the Spirit's supernatural empowerment remains essential in evangelism.

One young Christian, whose story I can personally verify, prayed with perhaps fifty people to accept Christ before he left for college. But while doing maintenance work at some apartments during one summer vacation, he began to discover more of this picture of Spirit-empowered evangelism in Acts. He decided to step out in faith the next chance he got. Once during the next few weeks, he prayed for someone, but as far as he knows nothing happened. However, during the same period, an older woman came by complaining that her doctors had been unable to do anything about her knee. With her permission he prayed over it. A few days later she returned, announcing that her knee had been better since he prayed and asking if he would please pray for her lungs now. "I've been coughing up blood, and my doctor thinks I have lung cancer," she lamented. So on his lunch break he went by her apartment. He began by explaining that whether or not God answered his prayer to heal her, she would die someday and therefore needed to be ready to meet Christ. After she prayed with him to submit her life to Christ, he prayed for her healing. She quit coughing up blood, and the doctor gave her a clean bill of health (though both the student and doctor warned her to quit smoking!); she lived about fifteen more years. Offering prayers of faith for people at work is hardly the same as emptying the wings of hospitals, but for this young man it was a start in building on the principle we find in Acts: when people see that God cares about their desperate situations, they often become more ready to pay attention to the rest of what God wants to do in their lives.

In Acts, God's Spirit empowered his church to evangelize the world, whether by signs or with boldness to speak, or both. Can anyone think that we need his power any less to complete the task in our generation? We should note, however, that in response to the hardships of their time, early Christians *sought* this continuing empowerment in prayer (4:29–31). If we lack such power, it may be in part because we have not sought it or because we have sought it only for our self-aggrandisement rather than for the evangelization of the world.

Are All Biblical Spiritual Gifts for Today? (Paul)

Paul treats the *charismata*, or "grace-giftings," in several different contexts, but all the relevant passages associate these gifts with members of the body of Christ. Whereas ancient culture recognized the idea of some exceptionally holy men who had power with God or with gods, Paul claims that every believer has a special relationship with God and specific assignments from God. This is significant because it means that for Paul *all* Christians are charismatic—endowed with special gifts to build up others. As Schatzmann puts it, Paul characteristically "regarded all the communities of believers as charismatic communities. He did not give the slightest indication that he knew of charismatic and noncharismatic churches."[6] Neither does he provide the slightest indication that he expects the cessation of any particular gifts (as opposed to others, like pastors or teachers, that we all recognize must remain today).[7] Three of Paul's surviving letters address gifts, always in the context of the body of Christ (Rom. 12; 1 Cor. 12; Eph. 4; compare 1 Peter 4:10–11).

Romans

In his letter to the Christians in Rome, Paul addresses a church experiencing tensions between Jewish and Gentile Christians. He begins his letter by laying the theological groundwork for reconciliation. Jewish people believed that they were automatically saved by virtue of their descent from Abraham and that they were special because they kept the law. Therefore Paul shows that

> all people are equally sinners (Rom. 1–3);
>
> spiritual, rather than ethnic, descent from Abraham is what counts (Rom. 4:1–5:11);
>
> all people (Abraham's descendants included) are descended also from Adam the sinner (Rom. 5:12–21);
>
> the law by itself cannot deliver from sin (Rom. 7:7–25);
>
> God can sovereignly choose people for salvation on grounds other than their ethnicity (Rom. 9);
>
> a sense of spiritual history prohibits Gentile Christians from looking down on Jewish people (Rom. 11).

Having established the theological point that Jew and Gentile must approach God on the same terms, Paul turns to his pastoral concerns. Believers must serve one another (12:4–16), the central focus of the law is loving one another (13:8–10), and Gentile Christians should not look down on Jewish Sabbath-keeping and food practices the way non-Christian Greeks and Romans do (Rom. 14). Both Christ (15:7–12) and Paul himself (15:15–32) become examples of reconciliation between Jew and Gentile, and Paul's concluding exhortation is to avoid those who cause division. Thus Paul discusses spiritual gifts (12:4–8) in the broader context of racial and cultural unity in the church. Although Paul had not visited the Roman church, he writes as if he expected them to be familiar with the gifts he lists. Part of his point may be that if many diverse members compose one body with regard to gifts, the same must be true of many diverse cultures in Christ's body. It is thus no coincidence that this particular list of seven emphasizes gifts for mutual service more than the lists in 1 Corinthians and Ephesians do.

In view of God's mercies in history recounted in Romans 9–11, Paul exhorts the Roman Christians to act as priests offering up sacrifices. The sacrifice they are to offer is to live the right lifestyle with their bodies, directed by a choice of their minds (12:1; the Greek literally speaks of a "rational" service, not a "spiritual" one). But granted that we should choose to use our bodies for God's glory, how does one know which specific role in God's plan to choose? A renewed mind will recognize God's purposes, knowing what is good in His sight (12:2). The renewed mind thinks not of oneself (12:3), but recognizes that all of us have special functions in Christ's body (12:4–8). In other words, in this context the living-sacrifice way to live uses the gifts God has given us to build up Christ's body and respects others' gifts no less. The gifts are essential for building up Christ's body, and as long as Christ's body needs to be built up, the gifts must continue to function for the body to be healthy.

1 Corinthians

Gifts may have been fresh on Paul's mind when he wrote his letter to the Romans because he wrote the letter from Corinth, a church that had some definite troubles with spiritual gifts. Like the Roman church, the Corinthian church was divided. But in this case, the division had more to do with social class than with ethnicity. Well-to-do Christians were concerned about what their social peers would think of their teacher. These well-to-do folk expected their teachers to be top-notch speakers and to depend on the financial support of their hearers. Instead, Paul embarrassed them by being a second-rate speaker—at least compared to Apollos (1 Cor. 1–4)—and by working as a common artisan for his support (1 Cor. 9). Paul's treatment of sexual issues (1 Cor. 5–7) may or may not have involved class tensions; intellectuals from various philosophic schools would justify free sex while avoiding marriage. The more educated members of the church also saw no problem with food offered to idols, as long as one knew that the idols were nothing; meanwhile, the well-to-do women saw no reason to wear traditional headcoverings to church (1 Cor. 8–11).

But besides all its other problems, the Corinthian church was abusing spiritual gifts. Apparently some Corinthian Christians were boasting that they could pray in languages unknown to themselves or their hearers. Paul puts tongues-speaking in its place, however, noting that the purpose of any gift in the public assembly was the building up of the church (1 Cor. 12:7; 14:1–5, 19). One could pray in tongues privately (14:18–19, 28; see 14:2–5), but it benefited others when practiced publicly only if someone interpreted (14:5, 13–17, 27–28). The Corinthians were also excited about wise and knowledgeable speech (1:5, 17), so Paul mentions these gifts as well (12:8). But Paul puts all the gifts in their place: if used in the public assembly, they were to be used only to serve the church.

As in Romans, Paul connects the gifts specifically to our Christian identity. We are members of Christ's body, each with our own roles as members of that body—hands, feet, and so on (12:15–26). Earlier writers had compared both the universe and the state to a body, but Paul may have been the first writer to speak of a religious group, God's people, in these terms. Paul is saying that each member has its function, and that we need each function. If any members are not functioning according to their gifts, the whole body suffers. One reason 95 percent of the work of the kingdom never gets done today is that 5 percent of the Christians are doing all the work, while the gifts of most of the body go unused. But if all members of the body remain essential today, all the gifts represented by those members are likewise essential.

That Paul assumes all gifts will continue until the return of Christ is clear from his argument in 1 Corinthians 13. There

Paul argues that love is more important than the gifts (13:1–3) and that love, in contrast to the gifts, is eternal (13:8–13). Paul mentions three representative gifts of special importance to the Corinthian Christians: prophecy, tongues, and knowledge (13:8), perhaps with slight emphasis on prophecy and knowledge (13:9). In the course of Paul's argument about the gifts being temporary, we learn when Paul expects them to pass away. The church will no longer need such gifts when we know as we are known (13:12; compare Jer. 31:34), which is when we see Christ face to face (13:12).

We live now in a time when we know Christ imperfectly, but when we see him face to face "the perfect" will come. The context leaves no doubt that "the perfect" arrives at Christ's second coming. Although some older interpreters argued that Paul's "perfect" referred to the completion of the canon, such an idea could not have occurred either to Paul or to the Corinthians in their own historical context (since at that point no one knew that there would *be* a New Testament canon).[8] Evidence from the context that "the perfect" refers to the second coming, together with the impossibility that Paul could have expected the Corinthian Christians to think he meant the canon, has left few evangelical scholars who continue to use this text to support cessation of the gifts. Gaffin, a prominent cessationist, concedes that "the view that they describe the point at which the New Testament canon is completed cannot be made credible exegetically."[9]

Elsewhere Paul compared the present revelation to a mirror (presumably of Corinthian bronze),[10] explaining to the Corinthian Christians that the Spirit reveals God's glory to believers no less fully than God revealed part of his glory to Moses on the mountain. Moses saw God "face to face" (Exod. 33:11; 2 Cor. 3:7–18); later Jewish teachers felt that other prophets, especially pagan prophets, saw less perfectly than Moses had (*Genesis Rabbah* 74.7; 91.6; *Leviticus Rabbah* 1.13–14). Paul believed that we see part of God's glory now; however, in 1 Corinthians 13 he points to the full revelation in the future when we will see perfectly.

Some have tried to use this passage to exclude some gifts before Christ's return, but their arguments cannot be judged successful. Prophecy and tongues must pass away when knowledge does, and if "knowledge" has passed away already, how can one "know" enough to say so? (On the meaning of "knowledge" in 1 Corinthians, see pages 112–13 below.) Nor can one keep knowledge and prophecy while discarding tongues. Prophecy in the biblical sense is no less dependent on spontaneous inspiration than tongues. It is not merely "preaching," since "sermons" in Paul's day involved especially the gifts of teaching and exhortation. One cannot make the verbs describing prophecy, tongues, and knowledge mean different things, so that tongues must pass away quickly while prophecy and knowledge remain until the end (as some interpreters have suggested). Paul uses different terms here for the sake of variation, as he often does. But even if one were tempted to make the terms mean something different, nothing would make one term suggest that tongues had passed away earlier—nothing, that is, except the need of an interpreter to make the passage say that. Various passages in the early church fathers indicate that they were aware of the continuance of supernatural gifts in their own time, despite the decline of some public gifts as authority became centralized in institutional leadership (see, for example, Justin Martyr *Dialogue with Trypho* 35; 82; 85; Tertullian *De Spectaculis* [*The Shows*] 26).

Jack Deere, a former cessationist professor who was forced to reexamine his position when he encountered modern miracles, provides six reasons in 1 Corinthians 12–14 alone that refute cessationism. In his popular but biblically and theologically informed response to cessationism, *Surprised by the Power of the Spirit,*[11] he points out that the gifts are for the common good (12:7), God commands us to zealously pursue spiritual gifts (12:31; 14:1), Paul warns us not to prohibit speaking in tongues (14:39), Paul valued tongues (14:5, 18), and spiritual gifts are necessary for the health of the body of Christ (12:12–27). Would God place such commands in Scripture if they were relevant for only about four decades, especially since during most of that time the majority of ancient Christians would not yet have had access to Paul's letter? Finally, Deere notes, Paul is explicit that these gifts will not cease until Christ's return (13:8–12).[12]

My own exegesis over the years has led me to the same basic conclusions. Deere and I are both experientially charismatic, so some could accuse us both of exegetical bias. But as he forcefully reiterates throughout his book, those who argue for an anticharismatic position are experientially noncharismatic—and Deere himself started as anticharismatic. The accusation of bias can be leveled either way, but I believe that cessationism would not naturally occur to someone reading the biblical text who had not already been taught the position or did not have an experiential bias that demanded it.

Merely Correcting Abuses?

Since Paul mentions tongues only in 1 Corinthians 12–14, where he is correcting abuses, some writers think that he regards tongues negatively. This view misses the point of Paul's argument. Paul himself prayed in tongues *privately* more than all the Corinthians, though he did not make a big deal about it (1 Cor. 14:18). Although the abuses in the Corinthian church require him to emphasize that tongues be kept in their place and be offered in proper order (14:40), he qualifies his words lest anyone overreact on the other side: he forbids the church to prohibit tongues in their public worship services (14:39). Paul would hardly add this warning against forbidding tongues if forbidding tongues were actually what he wished to do! If Paul guards against too negative a view of tongues even when he is correcting an abuse of the gift, how much less negative would he have been where no abuse existed?

Paul is instead addressing motives and public order: the public use of uninterpreted tongues is not helpful to the gathered church. Not only with regard to tongues, but with regard to other gifts and practices as well, many churches today would do well to heed Paul's admonition that "the spirit of the prophet is subject to the prophet" (1 Cor. 14:32–33). Although God may allow us more of a particular gift than we need, we must be prepared to limit our expression even in the gift of prophecy (14:29–33). In the same way, I might be able to teach from Scripture for ten hours straight, but this does not mean that God wants me to do so. Indeed, I *love* to teach for hours on end, but most students can only absorb teaching for so many hours in a row. (A recent Bible study with some students from a nearby Black college was an exception; we unexpectedly met for eight hours straight, finishing at 3 A.M. But that was because they did not want to stop!) The need of the church, rather than simply the availability of divine inspiration, should determine the use of any spiritual gift.

Although Paul corrects the abuse of tongues only in 1 Corinthians, this hardly means that tongues were practiced only in Corinth. First, Paul prayed in tongues regularly (14:18) and seems to have regarded prayer in tongues as a special form of prayer, "praying with one's spirit" (14:14–15). Second, Acts suggests to us that tongues evidenced divine inspiration in many early Christian communities, though Paul has occasion to address it only in the one congregation that is abusing the gift, Corinth. Third, we know that many of the gifts that Paul lists in 1 Corinthians 12 were standard practice in Paul's churches. Although his letters focus primarily on abuses and issues of local concern, it is clear that he expected prophecy to occur regularly (1 Thess. 5:20). His expectation should not surprise us since his Jewish contemporaries believed that prophecy would accompany the restoration of the Spirit. Finally, it is true that were it not for the Corinthians' abuse of tongues, we would know little about it in Paul's churches. But were it not for their abuse of the Lord's Supper, we would not be aware that any of Paul's churches practiced it. Paul's letters normally address specific situations, and we read them to learn both about how Paul dealt with these situations and about the faith and experience of the earliest Christians, information that is often assumed rather than articulated by Paul and his audiences.

Ephesians

Richard Gaffin rests his biblical case for the cessation of particular spiritual gifts almost entirely on Ephesians 2:20. On the basis of this text he contends that apostles and prophets—hence the gifts of apostleship, prophecy, and tongues (the latter being subsumed under prophecy)—were foundational. Hence they were no longer needed after the completion of the New Testament canon.

Gaffin is correct that in this context early Christian apostles and prophets performed a revelatory function (Eph. 3:5). One wonders, however, whether the need to make the revelations known might remain (see 3:8–13) and also whether other apostles and prophets might arise besides those in the foundation. After all, Paul here seems to refer to Christian prophets, rather than to ancient Israelite prophets, as part of the foundation (3:5; 4:11). Yet prophets had existed from early in Israel's history. Perhaps there are prophets that Paul does not mention here. Gaffin would argue that the completed canon obviates the need for further apostles and prophets, but surely he recognizes that Old Testament prophets did more than write Scripture. A survey of the prophets mentioned in the historical books of the Old Testament will reveal that most of them, in fact, did not write Scripture. Further, Paul's apostolic mission did not end when he made his gospel known to *someone;* the mission was to make it known to *everyone* (3:8–9). And to top it all off, Gaffin seems to read too much into the foundation metaphor of 2:20. Like the authors of the Dead Sea Scrolls, Paul and Peter portrayed their community of faith by the image of a temple. But pressing chronology into the image, so that all parts of the foundation must belong to the first generation, may be making Paul's illustration more specific than he intended. Examined from a number of angles, Gaffin's hypothesis falls quite short of adequate proof.

Gaffin's argument at this critical point, though using exegesis (Bible interpretation), is not strictly exegetical. He starts with a logical argument, to which he then adds the exegesis of texts that would not by themselves support his argument. While any "logical argument" looks consistent from within the system that supports it, it will fail to persuade those outside the system because it depends on other elements within the system to support it. This is the sort of objection that biblical scholars often raise against some systematic theologians or against other biblical scholars that they feel are too beholden to particular theological presuppositions. As Fee observes concerning the heart of Gaffin's argument for cessation,

> The logic *precedes* the exegesis. Indeed, the whole enterprise has its logical form structured by asking a question to which not one of the biblical texts intends an answer. Gaffin's overruling question is, *When* will tongues cease? The one text that addresses that question at all—and even there it is quite incidental to Paul's real point—is 1 Corinthians 13:10, which almost certainly intends, "at the Eschaton," as its answer. But since the answer is the one Gaffin is uncomfortable with, he sets up his logical circles to answer his own question with, "at the end of the first century." But in no case does he, nor can he, show that the answer to that question is a part of the biblical author's intent in the texts that are examined.[13]

At any rate, the analogy from Ephesians 2 provides a weak foundation for a doctrine of cessation, when the implications of other texts, including Ephesians 4, militate against it.

In Ephesians 4 Paul again addresses the unity of Christ's body (4:3–5). Although he approaches gifts as members of Christ's body from a very different angle than he approaches them in Romans and 1 Corinthians, he has not completely changed the subject. In this context, he still applies language familiar to us from Romans 12 and 1 Corinthians 12 ("measure," "grace"). He declares that God has distributed "grace" (as in "grace-gifts," *charismata*) to each member of the body, providing each one a special portion of the gift of Christ. Paul presumably means that the members of Christ's body carry on the non-atoning aspects of Jesus' own ministry (4:7; but see also the interpretation in the NIV, where Paul's phrase "the gift of Christ" is understood to mean "the gift *from* Christ" rather than "the gift *belonging to* Christ"). After introducing the subject of the gracious gift of Christ, Paul paraphrases a psalm that speaks of a triumphant ruler receiving and distributing plunder to his followers (Eph. 4:8). In Romans and 1 Corinthians, Paul writes that God has endowed each believer with special grace. However, in this passage Paul emphasizes another kind of gift first. Here the first gifts the exalted Christ gives to his body are a special group of persons who will in turn mobilize the other members of Christ's body for their ministries.

Christ provides ministers of his word in various forms, mostly (though not exclusively) for his church (4:12): apostles, prophets, evangelists, and pastor-teachers (4:11). These four designations do not necessarily exclude one another. Paul functioned as a prophet and teacher before beginning his apostolic mission (Acts 13:1). Long afterward he continued to function as a prophet (1 Cor. 14:37–38) and a teacher (1 Tim. 2:7; 2 Tim. 1:11). At least in the early church of Antioch, prophets and teachers seem to have filled the role of overseers (pastors; Acts 13:1); and in later Pauline churches, at least some elders (pastors) were prophetically endowed (1 Tim. 4:14). Timothy is both teacher (2 Tim. 2:24) and evangelist (2 Tim. 4:5). And one cannot read Acts 13–28 without recognizing that Paul is as much an itinerant evangelist as Philip had been in his earlier days. Obviously, these ministry callings can overlap. Nevertheless, we will attempt to summarize the basic sense of these offices.

First, Paul speaks of *apostles*. Paul never restricted the use of God's "apostles" to the Twelve or to the Twelve plus himself (1 Cor. 15:5–7; Rom. 16:7; compare Acts 14:4). Given the need for apostles in bringing Christ's body to maturity (Eph. 4:12–13), he would certainly assume that this gift, like the others he mentions, would continue to function until Christ's return. Some writers today see New Testament apostles as missionaries, but although Paul was certainly a missionary, the mission to the Gentiles was his specific call. New Testament evidence for most other apostles is inconclusive; most apostles apparently remained in Jerusalem nearly two decades after Jesus' resurrection (Acts 15:4). The most we can say from such evidence is that some apostles were missionaries, "master builders" who strategized and laid the foundations for churches in new regions (1 Cor. 3:10).

The term and its usage may tell us something more about apostles, however. Although Paul sometimes uses the term in a more general sense ("apostles *of the churches,*" 2 Cor. 8:23), when used by itself the term represents special envoys or ambassadors of God. An apostle is literally a commissioned "messenger," similar to the ancient idea of a herald or the Jewish custom of the *shaliach*. As an appointed agent of the one who sent him, a *shaliach* was backed by the full authority of the one who sent him (to the extent that he accurately represented his commission). Jewish people sometimes viewed the biblical prophets as God's *shaliachim*, but the New Testament uses "apostle" in a somewhat more specific way. Although God had authorized the prophets to speak for him, God's mission gave special authority to some prophets such as Moses, prophetic judges (Deborah, Samuel), and leaders who raised up prophetic movements (Elijah and Elisha). Christ apparently commissions Christian apostles (in the specific sense of apostleship) with a higher rank than normal prophets in order to strategize and act with authority.[14]

Second, Paul addresses *prophets*, who focused on the prophetic word. The term "prophet" applied in general to anyone who spoke for God. In the broadest sense (as we saw in Acts 2:16–18) it could apply to all witnessing Christians (Rev. 19:10). But in Ephesians, Paul often couples "prophets" with "apostles" as contemporary expositors of God's mysteries found in the Bible (2:20; 3:5). Thus by "prophets" here, Paul may mean more than merely those who offered prophecies of encouragement (1 Cor. 14:31) or who told people where their lost donkeys were (1 Sam. 9:6–9, 20). He may refer in this case to those who provide divine direction and strategies for Christ's body in the world, revealing God's purposes so God's people can impact their generation in the wisest way. He probably refers to an office of recognized prophets (Acts 11:27; 13:1; 21:10) rather than to anyone who occasionally prophesies. If the church should receive the message of true prophets, it is only because they have been thoroughly tested and found faithful to the message of previous generations of apostles and prophets in the Bible. Although they held less administrative authority than apostles, the prophets' mission of revealing God's purposes left them second only to apostles (1 Cor. 12:28).[15]

The third group, *evangelists,* focused on the saving gospel. An evangelist was literally a "herald of good news," a "gospelizer." Evangelists thus served the church by announcing the word that brought people into the church to begin with (Eph. 1:13). They were front-line warriors, because the one piece of armor for advancing into enemy territory and the one offensive weapon are both related to the gospel (Eph. 6:15, 17). By their example, these gifted gospelizers probably also stirred others in the church to witness, thereby continuing to build up Christ's body. In contrast to the use of the term in some church traditions, biblical evangelists are not simply people who go from church to church stirring up church members for a week. Evangelists are those who take the gospel directly to the streets, to the nursing homes, to the campuses, and so on, bearing the direct message of Christ. If some of them do travel from church to church stirring up church members, it is not simply to teach them that they should witness but also to show them how to witness, for instance by taking some of them out to the streets.

Fourth, Paul's language in the Greek refers to *pastor-teachers* as a single calling, whose focus was expounding the word God had already provided in the Old Testament and the traditions about Jesus (now recorded in our New Testament). While all the above gifts overlap, pastors by definition must be teachers of God's word. The word "pastors" means "shepherds," those whom God had appointed to watch over the sheep and care for their needs, as with Israel's spiritual leaders (Ezek. 34:2–4). These shepherds were also called "overseers" (KJV: "bishops") and "elders" (Acts 20:17, 28; Titus 1:5–7; 1 Peter 5:1–4). Just as one could seek other spiritual gifts (1 Cor. 14:1), one could desire the office of an overseer (1 Tim. 3:1), provided one met the qualifications of being above reproach in the local community where one functioned as a church leader (3:2–7). Pastor-teachers apparently focused on explaining God's word and applying it to the needs of their church members.

Most strikingly, this passage indicates the purpose for all these kinds of ministers of the word: they were to equip all God's people for the work of ministry, so that by evangelism, teaching, and inspired guidance the church would become all it should be (Eph. 4:12–13). This means that the most important function of these ministers of the word was to mobilize the rest of Christ's body, because *all* Christians are called to be ministers. The places where Christians work and study and reside are their parishes. If we could mobilize all Christians to minister where they live, we would have an army to proclaim Christ, to meet the needs of our society, and to lay a better foundation for our society's ethics. Can we imagine the impact on the church, and thus on the world, if these ministry gifts began functioning the way they should? As long as this work remains incomplete in any generation, we will continue to need the apostles, prophets, evangelists, and pastor-teachers who Paul says were called for this purpose (4:11–13). The text provides no indication that Paul expected some of these gifts to be temporary, while other gifts continued.

Many Gifts, One Body

In the Romans 12 list, Paul includes "supernatural" gifts like prophecy (12:6, a gift Paul always ranks near the top) and "natural" gifts like teaching (12:7). Today some people suggest that verifiably supernatural gifts have passed away, but that natural gifts like teaching continue. This distinction, however, violates Paul's whole pattern of thought. The Christian worldview acknowledges that *everything* in our lives is ultimately "supernatural," because even the food on our table is a gift of God's providence. The grace-gift of teaching is not simply an intellectual exercise devoid of reliance on God's Spirit—an unsaved person could then possess the same "gift." Teaching is a special endowment of grace that is also, as 1 Corinthians 12:8–11 shows, a special empowerment of God's Spirit. I personally would hate to try to teach in either a church or a classroom without first acknowledging to God my dependence on his Spirit to help me articulate the biblical text's concepts accurately and convincingly!

Although we learn about some gifts like prophecy and teaching in Paul's other letters, Paul focuses in 1 Corinthians on particular gifts that are most relevant to their situation. The Corinthian culture prized speaking and reasoning abilities; speech contests even constituted a regular part of the nearby biennial Isthmian Games. Naturally Christians in Corinth prized gifts like "wise speech" and "knowledgeable speech." Paul's letter also informs us that they prized tongues, perhaps because it is (at least today) one of those gifts that comes with the least amount of work.

While we should not play down the significance of any gift God has for us, it is easy to focus so much on one gift that we are unaware of entire areas of spiritual experience in the Bible that are unrelated to that particular gift. Paul not only prayed in tongues (1 Cor. 14:18) but also experienced deeper revelations in the Spirit (2 Cor. 12:1). However, he preferred to reserve such experiences mainly for his private devotion and boasted instead in his sufferings and weakness in which God alone was glorified (2 Cor. 12:1–10).

When Ezekiel saw the awesome majesty of the Lord, he was so overwhelmed that he fell on his face before God (Ezek. 1:28), but the Spirit empowered him to withstand the glory of the revelation and so to receive what God had to say (Ezek. 2:1–2). The Spirit here both reveals the majesty of our God and equips us with God's message to our generation.

The diversity of the Spirit's work should not surprise anyone who has read the Old Testament. Although God's Spirit was active in the whole creation (Gen. 1:2; Ps. 104:30; 139:7; perhaps Job 33:4; Isa. 34:16; 40:7), the Old Testament especially associates the Spirit with prophecy (Num. 11:25–29; 24:2; 1 Sam. 10:6, 10; 19:20, 23; 2 Sam. 23:2; 1 Kings 22:24; 1 Chron. 12:18; 2 Chron. 15:1; 18:23; 20:14; 24:20; Neh. 9:30; Isa. 61:1; Micah 3:8; Zech. 7:12), revelations (Ezek. 2:2; 3:12, 14, 24; 8:3; 11:1, 5, 24; 37:1; 43:5) other speaking for God (Isa. 42:1; 44:1–5; 48:16; 59:21; see 43:10), and perhaps prophets' empowerment to do miracles (2 Kings 2:9, 15; compare 1 Kings

18:12). Yet this part of the Bible also shows the Spirit empowering people for various skills, including art and architecture
devoted to God (Exod. 31:3; 35:31; see 28:3) and military and
political leadership (Num. 27:18; Deut. 34:9; Judg. 3:10; 6:34;
11:29; 13:25; 14:6, 19; 15:14; 1 Sam. 11:6; 16:13–14; Isa. 11:2;
Zech. 4:6; perhaps Ps. 51:11). Sometimes prophetic empowerment evidenced empowerment for leadership (Num. 11:17,
25–26; 1 Sam. 10:6, 10). Paul reflects the same emphasis on
the diversity of the Spirit's works, although, as in the Old Testament, various forms of prophetic speech predominate.

One final warning: one reason many of us may not experience any particular gifts may be because we do not "pursue"
them as Paul commands (1 Cor. 12:31; 14:1). Paul wants the
church as a whole to seek gifts, so his exhortation may not mean
that God will necessarily grant every gift that every Christian
desires (12:11). Paul surely does not imply that all Christians
should exercise all the gifts (12:28–30). But God often grants
prayer requests, especially when Christians offer them for his
honor. Paul gives us some guidelines for what kinds of gifts God
may be most eager to give us.

Some translators render the verb in 1 Corinthians 12:31 as a
statement ("you desire") instead of a command ("desire"). But
the same word occurs in 1 Corinthians 14:1 (where it is clearly
a command), forming a literary frame around chapter 13. That
chapter defines which are the "best" gifts one should seek: those
that build up the church by love. In churches where prejudice
against the gift would not create division, prophecy certainly
contributes to the building up of the assembly and is thus among
the "best" gifts in such settings (14:1). Some writers object by
saying that the Bible does not give us models of people seeking
gifts, but this is not quite true. The Book of Acts is the only book
of New Testament narrative outside the Gospels, and it provides
no examples of seeking gifts (tongues came spontaneously with
the Spirit) and few examples of anything else outside Luke's

purview. But in the Old Testament, Elisha cleaved to his mentor, seeking Elijah's empowerment. And in the New Testament, when the Samaritans did not receive the gift of the Spirit immediately, apostles went to make sure they received (Acts 8:14–17). These experiences serve as a model (see appendix), implying that we should seek the same empowerment the early church had if we lack it. Just as we accepted the teaching of narrative on a matter that Paul's letters did not address, so here we should accept Paul's letters on a matter that the narratives do not often directly address.

That God is ultimately sovereign over the distribution of gifts (1 Cor. 12:7) is no reason not to seek the gifts. God is sovereign over our food too, but though he desires to provide it for his children (see Matt. 6:25–34) and wants us to seek his kingdom first (Matt. 6:9–10, 33), he expects us to pray for him to provide our food (Matt. 6:11; 7:7–11). Those who argue that we should never seek gifts, that God will give them whether we ask for them or not, may be sounding a note of false piety, like some complacent American churchgoers in the eighteenth and nineteenth centuries who reasoned, "God will save us if he has predestined us, so there is no point in us trying to do anything about it." The Bible teaches both God's sovereignty and our responsibility to pray. If God has stirred passion for him in our hearts, our seeking God is also a gift from him. God does not grant every request, but that is not a reason not to ask.[16]

A Closer Look at Spiritual Gifts in 1 Corinthians 12:8–10

Although some popular writers have argued that Paul's list of nine gifts in 1 Corinthians 12:8–10 is a complete list of "gifts of the Spirit," Paul uses similar language in other passages with differing lists. Paul's various gift lists (1 Cor. 12:28; 12:29–30; 13:1–2, 8–9; 14:26; Rom. 12:4–8; Eph. 4:11; see also 1 Peter

4:10–11) demonstrate that his lists are ad hoc—that is, he is making them up "on the spot"—and they vary considerably. He could have listed other gifts than those he listed, and even his first readers may not have guessed *exactly* what each of his examples meant. Paul mentions specific gifts in 1 Corinthians 12:8–10 that relate to the experience of the Corinthian Christians. He probably places tongues at the bottom of this list (12:10) precisely because many in the church were assigning it too important a role in comparison with the other gifts (13:1; 14:2–5).

But because so many writers and speakers have appealed to the gift list in this particular passage, we will survey the general meaning of these gifts. This is especially necessary given the varying ideas prevalent today about what these gifts are. The surmises of one writer become the next writer's information, and that writer's information becomes a movement's tradition. Although charismatic scholars tend to pay more attention to what Paul actually says than do most teachers on a popular level, many charismatics have adopted ideas about these gifts that are based on charismatic traditions rather than on clues from the whole letter in which the list appears. Some of the gifts in this list overlap with other gifts on the list (for example, healings, miracles, and probably faith). Paul may have spontaneously coined the names of some of these gifts for this Corinthian list (for example, "word of knowledge"). He explains other gifts, however, in much greater detail. Indeed, given their Old Testament background, one could write entire books on prophecy and healing.

The Word of Wisdom

When Paul speaks of an "utterance of wisdom" in 12:8, the Corinthian Christians should immediately understand his point. Their city's culture emphasized speaking ability (the Greek term for "word" can also be translated "utterance" or "rhetoric") as well as knowledge and wisdom. As mentioned above, they included speaking contests along with the athletic games they sponsored every other year. The local Christians, following their culture's lead, valued knowledgeable and wise speech, especially the lofty discourses of the sophists and the probing thoughtfulness of the philosophers. Indeed, at least part of the church was so excited about its wise and knowledgeable speech that its members preferred Apollos, the public speaker, to Paul (see 1 Cor. 1–4).

But while Paul affirms that they abound in spiritual gifts like speaking and knowledge (1 Cor. 1:5–7), he is not impressed. The true wisdom, he insists, is God's hidden wisdom, the message of the cross. God's power was revealed in Christ's weakness, a message that matches what Jesus called the mystery of the kingdom (1 Cor. 1:18–2:16). Perhaps exaggerating the inadequacy of his speaking skills (as was the custom), Paul emphasizes that the message that saved them was neither rhetorically nor philosophically profound. It was simply God's message of salvation in Christ. The "utterance of wisdom," then, may represent the revelation of divine mysteries, based on insight into God's purposes rather than on merely human reasoning. Similar language for insight into God's mysteries occurs in the Dead Sea Scrolls.

The Word of Knowledge

To their contemporaries, "knowledgeable utterances" would be the sort of extemporaneous speeches public speakers offered on a variety of subjects, primarily for the purpose of showing off. Many Christians in Corinth claimed to have special doctrinal knowledge from God that they assumed made them better than Christians who did not possess it. Paul rebuked them for their abuse of this gift (8:1–3). Like tongues and prophecy, knowledge will pass away (13:8) and is incomplete and sometimes inaccurate (13:9). The "word of knowledge," or ability to speak knowledge publicly, undoubtedly means imparting knowledge about God; in other words, the gift of teaching (as many other Pentecostal and charismatic scholars agree, for example Stanley Horton and J. Rodman Williams).

In more traditional charismatic usage, "word of knowledge" applies to a supernatural impartation of knowledge about some human need or situation. While this interpretation of the gift does not fit Paul's usage, such a gift appears frequently in Old and New Testament narratives (for example, 1 Kings 21:17–18; 2 Kings 4:27; 5:26; 6:12; Mark 2:8; Acts 14:9). Paul would probably have subsumed that gift under the heading "prophecy" or "revelation" (see 1 Cor. 14:26, 30).

As a young Christian in the late 1970s I regularly witnessed this gift of revelation in an interdenominational fellowship in Ohio called High Mill Christian Center. Although not a member there, I always happily invited non-Christians to midweek services there because the pastor regularly revealed what someone was struggling with at the time, and he was invariably right. On one occasion, a visitor who had been planning to commit suicide that evening became a Christian instead. While this is not what Paul means here by "word of knowledge," it is a valid form of the gift of prophecy (1 Cor. 14:24–25).

Faith

Faith energizes all the gifts. God provides all Christians with faith to fulfill their function in Christ's body (Rom. 12:3, 6). In this instance, however, Paul speaks of a particular endowment of faith, of the sort that moves mountains (1 Cor. 13:2). "Moving mountains" was a Jewish figure of speech for doing what was virtually impossible, and Jesus had promised that nothing would be impossible to those who exercised even the smallest amount of faith (Mark 11:23). Since God is the object of our faith, possessing this faith presupposes that we are acting on God's will rather than our own (1 Kings 18:36; 1 John 5:14). Although it would be ideal for all Christians to function at this level, Paul recognizes that some Christians are specially gifted with this kind of faith. Rather than looking down on Christians less gifted in this area, they should use their gift on behalf of others in Christ's body, by their example encouraging others to grow in faith.

Gifts of Healing

The plural probably signifies, as many charismatic commentators suggest, that the Spirit develops in different Christians the faith to pray for different kinds of ailments. While this would not rule out someone gifted to pray for any kind of infirmity—most of the first-generation apostles seem to have done so (Acts 5:15–16; 28:8–9)—many Christians gifted in healing are initially able to exercise special faith only for particular kinds of infirmities. Acts 8:7 may imply this, though it may instead represent merely a concrete sample of the works performed. This may suggest that the gift's continuance to the present day does not guarantee that every individual will be supernaturally healed, although God often works dramatic healings to meet the needs of his children or to draw attention to the gospel they proclaim.

Perhaps in certain settings mature Christians developed faith for this gift. Jewish Christians like James seem to have expected elders to be ready to pray the prayer of faith (James 5:14–15). Probably in Paul's churches whoever had the gift of faith for healings was to act accordingly. In biblical traditions about miracle-working prophets such as Elijah and Elisha, the wide diversity of miraculous phenomena suggests no necessary limitation to a person's faith except the assurance that the person act on God's will, an assurance that flourishes in the context of an intimate and obedient relationship with God. While we should trust that God will often heal and should follow our Lord's example of compassion toward the physically as well as emotionally and spiritually wounded (Mark 1:41; Matt. 9:35–36), we should also avoid assuming that anyone who is not healed is spiritually deficient (compare Job 12:5; 42:7–8). God does not always heal right away (Job 42:10; Gal. 4:13–14; Phil. 2:27; 2 Tim. 4:20), and sometimes, for whatever reason, God does not choose to heal in this life (1 Kings 1:1; 2 Kings 13:14, 20–21; 1 Tim. 5:23). But Jesus' willingness to heal all who came to him certainly challenges those who think healing is abnormal today, unless they wish to contend either that Jesus' character has changed or that his power in the world has declined.

I suspect that we may see fewer people healed today than we need to, a suspicion that troubles me for the sake of brothers and sisters in need. Scripture shows that in some cases Jesus wanted people healed but his disciples were spiritually unprepared to provide what was needed (Mark 9:18–19, 28–29; Matt. 17:16–17, 19–20). That is not always the case, but hopefully, in this gift as in others, we can grow in faith rooted in an ever deeper relationship with God (James 5:14–18).

Workings of Miracles

"Miracles" literally means "demonstrations of power," and the plural may signify diverse kinds of workings for different miracle workers, as in the case of healings.[17] In the Old Testament and in stories about Jesus that Paul had told the Corinthians, "miracles" could include healings and presumably included acts of faith like moving mountains (1 Cor. 13:2). This gift probably overlaps with "gifts of healing" and "faith" elsewhere in the list. But it undoubtedly includes other kinds of miracles as well, such as nature miracles. When his disciples woke him from a nap to calm an apparently life-threatening storm, Jesus reproved their unbelief. Perhaps he was demanding why they did not act as he had taught them, instead of waking him with their fear (Mark 4:40). Certainly he questioned whether they could really have expected the boat to sink with Jesus in it. Similarly, another early Christian writer uses Elijah's faith to control rain according to God's will as an example for believers (James 5:17–18). James applies the example especially to faith for healing (5:14–16).

Probably the term more customarily refers to a standard sort of "demonstration of power" attested in Acts, such as exorcisms from demonized unbelievers (Acts 5:16; 16:18).

God, who sustains the universe by his power, regularly performs works without human vessels, but also often chooses to perform them through his servants. Thus, for example, a prophet confronts King Jeroboam, who, like stubborn Pharaoh of old, must be disciplined by a sign (1 Kings 13:1–6). The next recorded time Jeroboam hears a prophet, however, it is Jeroboam who initiates contact rather than the reverse, because his son is dying (14:1–3). God gets people's attention either directly or through his servants. For example, God often speaks through judgments (Isa. 26:9–10), but usually sends prophets first to interpret the judgments (Amos 3:7–8; Isa. 48:3–5).

In any case, those gifted to work miracles should remember that miracles come in response to *God's* command (1 Kings 18:36) or the prayer of someone walking close to him (2 Kings 1:10), not simply our self-centered desire (compare James 4:1–4). Those whose desires are granted are those who delight in God and desire his will supremely (Ps. 37:3–7). Acting on a word from the Lord is not the same thing as "confessing" or "claiming" that something should happen, as if we ourselves, rather than God, have authority to speak things into being (Lam. 3:37; Rom. 4:17). We should also recognize that for the edification of the body of Christ, gifts related to God's word are ranked higher than this spectacular gift (1 Cor. 12:28).

Prophecy

Those who think that prophecy in 1 Corinthians 12–14 is merely preaching must treat as irrelevant the Old Testament use of the term (the background Paul shared with his Christian readers), the use in Acts, and the use in the text itself. Prophecy may "reveal the secrets of hearts" (14:24–25) and may be spontaneous revelation (14:29–31). Prophets could, of course, "preach." In fact, the biblical terminology for prophecy is broad enough to include any message that the prophet received from the Lord and made clear was from God. God spoke to his people through prophecy from the very start, but prophecy came in a variety of forms: visions, dreams, audible voices, ecstatic trances, and probably most often the Spirit bringing words to the heart and/or mouth of the prophet. Some texts even attest prophets receiving messages by prophesying to themselves (2 Sam. 23:2–3; Hosea 1:2; possibly also Jer. 25:15; 27:2). Prophetic inspiration came in such a variety of forms that one could easily move back and forth between prayer or worship and prophecy (for example, 1 Chron. 25:1–8; Ps. 12:1, 5; 46:1, 10; 91:3, 14–16). In fact, worship often set the tone or provided the context for prophecy (1 Sam. 10:5; 2 Kings 3:15; possibly also Hab. 3:19).

The distinguishing feature of such prophecy is not the form used, but whether the word of the Lord is being proclaimed. Although most of the Old Testament prophetic books focus on prophecies to God's people or to other groups, prophets delivered countless prophecies to individuals. Due to their focus, the Old Testament books often record personal prophecies to kings, but less-prominent persons also received messages (for example, 1 Kings 17:13–14; 2 Kings 4:3–4). Texts like 1 Samuel 9:6–10 indicate that individuals also customarily inquired of prominent prophets. Acts records personal prophecies to Paul (Acts 21:4, 11; compare 20:23).

Before the Exile most prophets who recorded their prophecies prophesied in poetry; after the Exile, most prophecies were in prose (for example, most of Haggai and Malachi). Nor must prophecies by nature be only spontaneous, as some have argued. Often biblical prophets received a prophecy at one time but delivered it later (Jer. 28:12–17), and a prophet could even record his prophecy and allow another to read it later (Jer. 36:4–8).

While all inspired speech is "prophetic speech" in the broadest sense of the term (compare, for example, Acts 2:4, 16–18; Rev. 19:10), by "prophecies" Paul specifically means revelatory words, in this case spoken in a congregational setting. He did not confuse the gift with teaching (expounding Scripture or the implications of the gospel), although one may learn from prophecies (1 Cor. 14:31). Nor did he confuse it with "exhortation" as a discrete gift (Rom. 12:8; Paul uses the gift in Rom. 12:1), although prophecy likewise could include this function (1 Cor. 14:3). In teaching, God's authority rested in the text or other prior message and was appropriated by the teacher to the extent that the teacher accurately expounded it. In prophecy, God's authority was in the prophecy itself to the extent that the prophecy accurately reflected what the Spirit was saying (although New Testament prophecy, like Old Testament prophecy, often reflected the language of earlier biblical prophecies). In prophecy, one was inspired to speak directly as God's agent, essentially declaring "Thus says the Spirit" (Acts 21:11; Rev. 2:1; 3:1).[18]

Although Paul seems to have known of experienced prophets who spoke God's message (Acts 11:28; 21:10; Eph. 4:11), in 1 Corinthians he employs the term "prophet" more broadly to describe all those who prophesy (1 Cor. 14:29–32). In theory, at least, because all Christians have received the Spirit, all Christians can prophesy (14:5, 31), though in practice not all will do so (12:29). Prophets may, however, function on different levels. We may appreciate the prophecies of encouragement, which seem common today, but unfortunately there remains a dearth of prophets who will stand for God's ideals of justice against the oppression of the poor and powerless elements of society. Reflection on this emphasis in biblical prophecy (for example, Isa. 1:15–17; 58:1–14; Jer. 22:13–17; Amos 5:7–24; James 5:1–6) might broaden the scope of contemporary prophecy.

Discernment of Spirits

Although modern readers employ this phrase in a variety of ways, the context indicates that Paul meant especially the gift of evaluating prophecy accurately. This is not to say that being able to detect error in nonprophetic situations is not from the Spirit. (I have on occasion met persons and known by the Spirit that they were in a particular cult or false teaching before they provided any tangible indication of it.) But Paul specifically refers to evaluating prophecies. He later uses the same Greek word for "discerning" in this manner (14:29) and elsewhere speaks of "spirits" in conjunction with prophecy (14:32; see also perhaps 1 John 4:1–6; Ezek. 13:3; Rev. 22:6).

In the Old Testament period, experienced prophets often mentored the prophetic development of novices (1 Sam. 19:20; 2 Kings 2:15; 4:38). Among first- and second-generation Christians, maturing prophets had to mentor one another by evaluating one another's prophecies (1 Cor. 14:29). Like our teaching, our prophecies are not perfect or complete, for we all "know in part and prophesy in part" (1 Cor. 13:9). Feeling moved by the Spirit with the burden of God's message is not the same thing as writing canonical Scripture. Indeed, most prophecies in biblical times were not recorded in Scripture (for example, 1 Kings 18:13). Further, human error can interfere in our prophecy—even apostles could be mistaken in some assertions or actions (Gal. 2:11–14). But God builds a safety mechanism into the church's use of prophetic gifts by warning us that human error can distort them and by requiring us to test all our finite assurances that the Spirit is speaking to us. That is why prophecies must be tested (1 Thess. 5:20–22), not quenched (1 Thess. 5:19). Both those who do not evaluate the claims of ones who say they've heard from God and those who uncritically reject all supernatural revelations equally disobey Scripture (1 Cor. 14:39–40).

Some people who prophesy today simply use stereotypical phrases and prooftexts out of context; some may simply be trying to prophesy without first developing a relationship with the God of Scripture. In other cases, perhaps such weak prophesiers feel the Spirit's inspiration but are not yet full enough of biblical revelation to translate those feelings into a more accurate understanding of what God is saying. Rather than assuming that they have no evidence of the gift of prophecy, we should encourage them to immerse themselves in Scripture and be mentored by the prophecies of God's Word interpreted in their proper context and with sensitivity to their cultural background. The language of the biblical prophets is rich with allusions to earlier prophets and especially to the Mosaic covenant. Perhaps even the false prophets of Jeremiah's day could have been turned to the truth and led others in that direction had they genuinely learned to hear God's voice and proclaim the unpopular message God had for his disobedient people (Jer. 23:21–22).

But all prophecy must be tested by Scripture and, where that is impossible because of the subject matter of the prophecy, by other mature and Bible-centered prophets sensitive to the Spirit (1 Cor. 14:29). The most sensitive believer still has more to learn about sensitivity to the Spirit's voice and must submit to Scripture—understood in context—as the "canon," the measuring stick and final arbiter of revelation. To fail to do so is arrogance and invites the discipline of the Lord. Can we possibly think that any one of us hears God accurately if we contradict the apostles and prophets God inspired through the centuries, whose prophecies were tested by time and were fulfilled? When those who prophesy apply Scripture according to teachings circulating only in their own charismatic circle rather than according to the Scripture's context, our guard should go up.

Various Kinds of Tongues and Interpretation of Tongues

The public function of tongues, like its private function, seems to have been prayer and praise (1 Cor. 14:14–17; see also Acts 2:11; 10:46).[19] Whether in a language one did or did not know, Paul regarded prayer as too important to be done without the Spirit's inspiration and empowerment (see also Eph. 6:18; Jude 20). Biblical evidence for tongues functioning as a message from God, perhaps to the individual (1 Cor. 14:28), is possible yet remains inconclusive. This is not to say that God could not sovereignly use public utterances in tongues differently today than in the Bible, even if this meant choosing to accommodate human tradition to communicate his will. Pentecostal theologians still debate the matter, but I see no reason why God could not at least on occasion do so. The biblical emphasis of tongues, however, is clearly on Spirit-led prayer.[20]

Although Paul thinks that tongues would be good for everyone, he insists that prophecy would be better (14:5). Tongues is valueless except for the person whose spirit is praying, unless that person or someone else interprets and makes tongues intelligible for the gathered body (14:13–19). The principle Paul uses here extends beyond tongues. In the gathered assembly, we should make sure that any contributions we bring—whether supernatural gifts or a song or a sermon—are worth the time of those who must listen to us. If what we bring is for our good alone, we may as well offer it in private. Paul does not prohibit interpreted tongues, but he restricts uninterpreted tongues entirely to the context in which his own use of the gift occurs: private prayer (14:28; compare 14:18–19). Perhaps Paul would not have objected to a prayer meeting in which many were speaking under inspiration simultaneously, as described in 1 Samuel 10:5–6 and 19:20, but he objected to anything that would dis-

tract the assembly from its chief purposes for gathering: edification, exhortation, and evangelism (14:3, 23–25).

Although in 1 Corinthians 12–14 Paul focuses on gifts for
the building up of the church (hence his insistence that tongues
in public be interpreted), we will briefly digress to investigate
the private use of tongues. Those of us who usually minister in
churches where the public use of tongues would probably
divide more than edify, tend to be more comfortable in practice with the private use of tongues. Nevertheless, according
to Paul tongues is a valid public gift, when interpreted, once
churches understand and appreciate its function. Paul indicates that tongues is prayer with one's spirit (14:14–16) and
that it edifies the person praying (14:4). Edifying oneself is not
a sub-Christian goal, even if it is not the goal of ministry in the
church (see, for example, Jude 20). Do we not pursue personal prayer and Bible study partly to strengthen our own relationship with the Lord?[21] Paul would not mind if everyone
prayed in tongues, though prophecy is more valuable because
it edifies the whole church (14:5). Although in public, uninterpreted tongues serve no function, and Paul seems reticent
to pray publicly in tongues, he nevertheless prays in tongues
quite a bit—undoubtedly in his private devotional life
(14:18–19). He may also have chosen to interpret these utterances in order to edify his mind (hence "praying with the
understanding" in the context of 14:13–16).

In contrast to some Pentecostals, I believe that "tongues" in
both Acts and 1 Corinthians refers to genuine languages unknown
to the speaker. I believe that tongues should be the same today,
though Vern Poythress and D. A. Carson may well also be right
about the encoding of the language.[22] I am not suggesting that
Pentecostals police one another to make sure the words *sound*
like a genuine language; I have heard real foreign languages that
sound like perfect gibberish to me. We also have to allow those
who are young in a gift to mature in their use of it, as with

prophecy or teaching or any other gift. The speakers' focus should be on sincerely praying with their spirit to God, allowing the Holy Spirit to make sure the words come out right. Yet some tongues-speakers do seem to perform their "gift" out of habit or rote, rather than by cultivating sensitivity to the Spirit. When one hears a particular phrase (for example, the rather common "shonda ma kee") repeated some ten times and followed by a much more lucid "interpretation," one is tempted to be rather skeptical concerning the "tongue." Believing in the reality of the genuine gift does not require us to accept as genuine all purported manifestations of the gift. Jonathan Edwards warned of spiritual counterfeits during genuine times of revival, and William Seymour argued that one who focused on signs more than on God and his holiness would get a counterfeit. Of course, I intend this observation to move us to seek a deeper sensitivity to the Spirit, not to cause sincere but insecure seekers to doubt the reality of their experience.

Today some segments of Christendom emphasize the mind to the exclusion of other aspects of the human personality; other groups emphasize emotion to the exclusion of reason. Tongues are not primarily rational; those of us who emphasize rationality in other aspects of our faith may especially need the kind of emotional release tongues provide. To illustrate the value of "praying with one's spirit," even when one does not immediately comprehend what one is praying, I'd like to tell a story I know firsthand (the characters must remain anonymous to protect the father's identity).

A seminary student got into a loud debate with his hermeneutics professor over the interpretation of a verse in Philippians, and for the rest of the day he felt incomprehensibly threatened. He knew he needed to apologize to the professor, but why was the debate bothering him so much? He began to pray in tongues, and as his spirit prayed, his mental defense mechanisms could not suppress his true feelings from coming out. As he poured out his heart in tongues, the Spirit also began to provide the interpretation for what he was feeling. He realized that he felt threatened by authority figures because he had always felt threatened by his father, the one authority figure he had experienced in his formative years. As long as he could remember, his father had always ridiculed whatever he would say, no matter how hard he sought to defend himself with valid arguments. As the buried feelings continued to pour forth in a language he could not interfere with, he realized something that he never would have verbalized: he had hated his father. As he continued to pray, however, he began to weep, realizing how much he had loved his father too.

The next day he apologized to his professor, who also apologized to him and declared, "But now we'll be better friends for it. From now on, call me 'Gary,'" (the professor's first name). The professor was a godly Christian man, but the seminarian still had to deal with his father, who was not a Christian, and with whom he had never in his life had an intimate conversation. He began praying about resolving his relationship with his father, and that summer, for the first time in a few years, he traveled to see his father. One afternoon, when the other family members were out of the house, he found his father reading a newspaper. "Dad, may I speak with you?" he asked. Even trying to open the subject was difficult.

"Sure, son," his father responded, the newspaper still in front of his face.

"Dad, what I'm about to tell you—I'm not saying that you were like this, just that this was my perception of you growing up. Dad, I never felt I could talk with you about anything. I felt like you never listened to anything I had to say, and I felt I hated you for that. But I want to let you know that I'm really sorry for having felt that way, because I really love you now."

With the paper still in front of his face, his father responded, "That's all right, son. That's how every kid feels about his dad."

But the young man knew that he himself had done what was required of him.

Later, the seminarian's mother asked him what he'd spoken with his father about that day. "He's been acting differently ever since then," she observed, noting that he was now spending time with his youngest son who remained at home. When he told his mother what his father had said, she responded, "That's how he felt about *his* father. But he never made peace with him before he died."

Because of a prayer from his spirit, the seminarian was able to resolve some emotional conflicts that he might never have admitted he had. He was able to break a transgenerational cycle of pain because his spirit could be honest about feeling something his mind had not wanted to admit.

Gifts as Initial Evidences of Apostleship?

Before moving from the discussion of the continuance of spiritual gifts, we must address one more objection not included above because we restricted our argument primarily to Pauline passages. Hebrews 2:3–4 indicates that God confirmed the message of the first witnesses with signs and gifts of the Spirit, and from this some have inferred that these signs and gifts had ceased by the time the author of Hebrews was writing. If this argument were correct, it would actually prove too much for most of its proponents; it would suggest that God does no miracles today!

But the argument is inadequate to carry even the minimum weight placed on it. The author of Hebrews is warning that since the gospel of Christ is a greater revelation than the law, those who neglect it will face greater penalty (Heb. 2:1–3). God had confirmed the message with notable signs in the past (2:4), but this no more suggests that God had stopped working signs than it suggests that the gospel would no longer be preached. The verb for God's bearing witness with signs is simultaneous with the verb for Christ's first witnesses preaching about him. In both cases it refers to the time when the Hebrews received the gospel. If God's miraculous bearing witness has ceased, one could suggest in the same manner that the preaching of Christ has also ceased. Those who argue that God provided signs to attest Christ's witnesses may be right, but this is hardly the only purpose of signs in the New Testament. God is more often said to attest his *message*, not just the first witnesses to that message (for example, Acts 14:3), so it is reasonable to expect God to continue to use signs to confirm his message today. Nor do Paul's later letters indicate the disappearance of gifts, as some have thought (1 Tim. 1:18; 4:14; 2 Tim. 1:6). Someone not being healed (2 Tim. 4:20) was not a new phenomenon; some in an earlier period were not miraculously healed (Gal. 4:13–14; Phil. 2:27).

The Importance of Spiritual Gifts and Miracles Today

Although some have argued that miracles are limited to specific periods in biblical history, a simple survey of the Bible shows this argument to be mistaken.[23] Yet although there are more than three periods, and miracles are hardly limited to them, miracles do seem to cluster in certain generations in history, both in the Bible and subsequently. When one examines the Bible and church history, one quickly sees that the distribution of miracles is not random. Israel would often stray far from God until he raised up servants to lead them back to his law, a process repeated throughout history. Although not all God's servants worked miracles (Gideon, Jeremiah, and John the Baptist, for instance, did not), the raising up of true prophets especially preceded times of revival, and miracles and renewals of worship (see repeatedly in 1 and 2 Chronicles) often accompanied these times of revival.

Recognizing that God is sovereign over times of revival is not the same as supposing that we can do nothing to make ourselves more prepared for it. I believe the time has come for our generation to seek God's face, to ask him to perform his purposes in our societies today. Yet we must also be ready to allow God to do whatever must be done to answer that prayer—even if that means judgment and stripping from us the things we value, so we may learn to value what really matters. Our spiritual forebears prayed that God would embolden and empower his servants in proclaiming Christ by granting healings, signs, and wonders (Acts 4:29–30). (Although the NIV separates this into two sentences, the Greek favors the translation: "grant us boldness *by* stretching out your hand to heal" [compare KJV] or "*while* stretching out your hand to heal" [compare RSV, etc.]; see also Acts 14:3.) Signs and wonders provide a powerful attestation of God's power and interest in this world and summon people's attention to the gospel we proclaim.

More important and critical is the prayer for the Spirit's empowerment, however. In Luke's Gospel, the Lord's prayer for the coming of God's kingdom and deliverance from temptation is in a context of prayer that climaxes in entreaty for the ultimate gift: God's Spirit (Luke 11:1–13). In the context of Luke's emphasis on the Spirit, this is a prayer for empowerment so we can do the work that is a prerequisite for the final coming of the kingdom.

Conclusion

I have seen many miracles, but Scripture leads me to expect many more than I have seen. Although I have heard of miracles like those in Acts happening regularly in some other places, I frankly confess that I have not witnessed many miracles on that scale. I could seek theological rationalizations for this lack, contending that God simply does not want to do such miracles today, but seeking an argument to validate my experience would violate every principle of theological integrity I have worked to develop over the years. I am an evangelical who is convinced that Scripture is God's Word. I must submit to it rather than make it say what is convenient. As a biblical scholar who by conviction determines the meaning of the text first and then asks its implications for today, I must conform my experience to the Bible rather than the Bible to my experience. In other words, I remain charismatic because I am evangelical, rather than the reverse (even though my spiritual experience has often helped fortify my evangelical convictions while working through formidable liberal scholarship over the years). While it would be difficult now for anyone to convince me that miracles do not happen today, my understanding of each passage is negotiable: I just want to understand and obey what the biblical text says. The Bible's message does not simply confirm my own experience of miracles; it summons me to be more open to appropriate signs and wonders than I already am.

God has often renewed miracles in times of revival, sometimes performing those miracles through individuals like Moses, Elijah, or the apostles. God does not gift us all for the same tasks, but those of us with the gift of teaching must mobilize the whole body of Christ to use their scriptural gifts and not, as we have often done, merely train fellow teachers. God is sovereign and need not do a miracle simply because we request it. But if we acknowledge God as our sovereign, we must be available for him to work through our prayers if he does will to do a miracle. We must become stronger people of the Spirit whom God may empower by whatever means he chooses.

Our generation is in desperate shape. Those involved in inner city evangelism and other front-line ministries need firsthand faith in God's protection like the prophets Elijah or Elisha sought when facing grave dangers from mortal opposition. Some secu-

lar intellectuals have become disillusioned with their antisupernaturalism, but many are turning to superhuman forces infinitely
less powerful and benevolent than the God we serve. Perhaps it
is time for us in our generation to cry with the newly empowered Elisha, "Where now is the LORD, the God of Elijah?"
(2 Kings 2:14 NIV).

At the same time, we must seek the gifts with the right
motives. One can pray in tongues without living a Spirit-filled
life (compare the spiritually immature in 1 Cor. 14:20); one
can prophesy without being saved (1 Sam. 19:21–24; Matt.
7:21–23); one can utter charismatic praise songs without giving attention to God himself, celebrating the rhythm or melody
rather than our God's greatness (compare the mere religious
forms in Zech. 7:5–10).

One of the early pioneers in the mid-twentieth-century
healing revival believes that the beginning of that revival came
mostly from God's Spirit. Many of God's people had been
seeking his face, and when they sought his face he opened his
hand to bless them. But this same minister has concluded that
when God's people then turned from seeking his face to seeking his hand, he closed it again. From that time forward, most
of the "healing revival" was carried on in the flesh, with many
healing evangelists jockeying for attention and losing the blessing of God's Spirit. This leader warned that he believed God
would not open his hand in such a manner again until he had
raised up a generation of Christians who would not be cor-
rupted by money, sex, or power—a generation he believes is
finally beginning.

If God works miracles, the miracles must be for the honor of
God's name alone. God may use us in various gifts—such as
teaching, healing, evangelism, charismatic prayer, and
prophecy—but unless we first seek God's honor and work in
conjunction with all the other gifts for the building up of Christ's
church and its mission in this world, we are not behaving like

people of the Spirit. May God send us a revival of signs, wonders, and spiritual gifts. But most of all may God send us a revival of his Spirit that causes our hearts to feel God's heart, for the power of the Spirit (1 Cor. 2:4–5) lies not first of all in powerful signs, but in the message of the weakness of the cross (1 Cor. 1:18; 2:6–8). It is in our weakness, our absolute dependence on him, that we become vessels truly ready for his honor (2 Cor. 11:18–12:10; 13:3–4, 9).

How Can We Recognize the Spirit?

n Western Christianity today, issues like Spirit baptism and spiritual gifts are far more controversial than discussions about the Spirit's character, but perhaps for this very reason we have neglected to learn as much about the Spirit as we should. The Holy Spirit, like the Father and the Son, is not just a doctrine, an idea, or an experience to be tagged onto the other doctrines and experiences of our Christian life—he is the God who has invaded our lives with his transforming presence.

Many of us need guidance to recognize more accurately when and how the Spirit speaks. Some circles in the church tend to exclude the Spirit's work almost altogether, content to depend on human programs and abilities. As one preacher remarked, "Were the Spirit to be withdrawn suddenly from the earth today, most of the church's work would continue unabated." In other circles, nearly everything that happens is attributed to the Holy

Spirit, though much of what happens there has nothing to do with him.

In this chapter, therefore, we begin with the less controversial, but nevertheless crucially practical question, How can we recognize the Spirit? This question is vital and practical for two reasons. First of all, we need to recognize the Spirit in order to deepen our own personal relationship with him. Second, we need to recognize the Spirit so we can discern his true presence and activity in the church, as opposed to what sometimes passes as his presence and activity. After briefly commenting on the Spirit and his character as God, we will turn to two primary issues: How can we cultivate sensitivity to the Spirit's voice? and How can we cultivate the Spirit's character (fruit) in our lives?

Who is the Spirit?

Christians today agree on many details about the Spirit. We recognize that the Spirit is the third person of the Trinity (Father, Son and Holy Spirit). Early Christians recognized that his deity is the same as that of the Father and the Son, although each person of the Trinity differs from the other two in some of the work he does.

I must pause here momentarily to explain why we call the Spirit "he" rather than "it." The word for "spirit" is feminine in Hebrew, neuter in Greek, and masculine in Latin; hence pronouns for the Spirit are normally neuter in the Greek New Testament. (The exceptions are passages in John that refer to the Spirit as the "Paraclete," or counselor, a masculine term in Greek.) Nevertheless, we use the masculine pronoun for the Spirit here to remind readers that he is a person, an individual, not an impersonal force.

Although the New Testament certainly affirms the deity and personhood of the Spirit, we must recognize that these were not the points that New Testament writers usually emphasized. Perhaps because their Jewish contemporaries were less inclined to debate the personhood of the Spirit than, say, Christ's deity, the New Testament usually assumes, rather than defends, the distinct personhood of the Spirit (Matt. 28:19; John 14:16–17; 16:13–15; Rom. 8:26–27; 2 Cor. 13:13). Though Jewish teachers did not think of the Spirit as a distinct person, first-century Jews took for granted that the Spirit was deity (see, for example, Isa. 40:13; 48:16; 63:10–11; Acts 5:3–5). The New Testament instead primarily focuses on the Spirit's work in transforming and empowering believers. The very activity of God's Spirit among the Christians testified to their contemporaries that the promised era of the Spirit had come and, hence, that the Messiah had come!

The New Testament writers were interested in practical theology, and in two situations discussions of the nature of the Spirit become especially practical for us. First, in polemical or apologetic situations, we must explain the nature of the Spirit to those who misread New Testament assumptions and question the Trinity (for example, Jehovah's Witnesses). This was the situation under which Greek theologians later formulated their precise statements about the Spirit. Second, we wish to know more about the Spirit when we love God the Father, the Son, and the Spirit and yearn to know them better; we want what we know about God to help us better worship God. Because another volume in this series will focus on the Trinity, we here emphasize what we can know about the Spirit's ministry in practice.

Knowing the Spirit Personally

Some people suppose that "learning theology" means learning about God only in an abstract, rational sense, with little impact on their personal relationship with him. But when the Bible talks about knowing God, it speaks of a relationship characterized by intimacy and obedience, not by merely intellectual knowledge. Knowledge about God is clearly essential for knowing him, because a relationship with someone demands that we get to know about that person. But knowledge about God is inadequate unless we apply it practically to our relationship with him. In fact, merely knowing about him without applying that knowledge leads to more severe judgment (Luke 12:47–48; Rom. 2:12–16; James 3:1).

We should know and celebrate God with our whole person. While too many Christians neglect serving God with the mind, others cultivate only their minds and neglect the emotional aspects of worship. One need only begin to study the Psalms to realize that God touches the affective (emotional) dimension of the human personality as well as the intellect, and God expects us to worship with our whole being—not with our intellect alone.

To know the Holy Spirit involves more than knowing some facts about him. Knowing the Holy Spirit means pursuing a personal and intimate relationship with him. Because the Father, Son, and Spirit are one in nature (though distinct in person and role), what we learn about the character of one member of the Trinity applies to all three. Just as one cannot have a relationship with the Father except through the Son (1 John 2:23), one cannot have a relationship with the Son except through the Spirit (John 16:14; Rom. 8:9) or vice versa (John 14:17). Thus whatever we learn here about our relationship with the Father or the Son also applies to our relationship with the Spirit through whom we experience the presence of the Son and the Father. In this chapter we will examine how Christians can deepen their personal relationship with God through the Holy Spirit. We begin with comments on worship that the Spirit leads us to offer to God and then turn to the subject of how the Spirit can speak to us. We begin with worship because, more than any other activity with the possible exception of evangelism, worship can focus us on God's own glory.

Spirit-Empowered Worship

Acts reveals the character of Spirit-empowered *evangelism,* Paul's letters often focus on the importance of Spirit-empowered *behavior,* but the Bible also teaches us about Spirit-empowered *worship.* In the Old Testament, prophetic empowerment often helped believers worship God, and worship often deepened sensitivity to the Spirit's voice (for example, Exod. 15:20–21; 1 Sam. 10:5; 2 Kings 3:15; Hab. 3:19). Worshipful celebration of God's goodness was essential for all his people in the Old Testament (see 1 Chron. 6:31–32; 15:16, 28–29; 16:4–6; 23:27, 30; 2 Chron. 31:2; Neh. 12:24, 27, 36, 43), and the major revivals in Israel's history included revivals of worship (2 Chron. 8:14; 20:20–22; 29:25; Ezra 3:10–11). David himself appointed orderly but prophetically-inspired worship leaders in the tabernacle (1 Chron. 25:1–7). Many of the psalms originated in this Spirit-inspired worship (2 Chron. 29:30) and were perpetuated there (Neh. 12:45–46). God deserves worship that is no less Spirit-led today (John 4:24; Phil. 3:3).

Worship is not merely enjoying the rhythm of a song, experiencing an emotional feeling, or comprehending a liturgy. Nor is it repeating glib phrases without recognizing the one who deserves the phrase. When the psalmist declares, "Hallelujah!" or (in English) "Praise the Lord!" this is a strong Hebrew imperative: that is, it is an urgent, strong command, uttered by the worship leaders in the temple to the people who had come to worship. It is not so much worship itself as a call to worship!

Worship is giving the appropriate honor to God; it is an ultimate act of faith, where we acknowledge God's greatness directly to him. God often responded to such genuine worship and faith by acting on behalf of his people (for example, 2 Chron. 20:20–24). We need to glorify God and allow him to express his power among us today as well. As a royal priesthood (1 Peter 2:5, 9; Rev. 1:6), we must offer a more meaningful sacrifice than that of bulls and goats, offering both our lips and our hearts in magnifying God.

Our mission in this world involves bringing people from all cultures to exalt the name of Christ, even though we do not always see the responses we work for. Yet whatever the visible results on this side of eternity, our very labors fulfill part of our mission by glorifying God. God created us to bring him honor with both our lips and our lives, yet God is so great that only his Spirit working within us can create genuine, sincere praise appropriate to his majesty.

Early Christians recognized that the Spirit himself must empower us to offer praise worthy of a God greater than all his creation. They spoke of "worship in the Spirit" (John 4:24; Phil. 3:3; see also Eph. 6:18; Jude 20). Some passages provide glimpses into the early Christians' Spirit-led worship, which apparently included singing, sometimes in tongues not even known to the worshipers (1 Cor. 14:15; compare Eph. 5:18–20). God is no less great today than he was in the Old Testament and in the early church, and no less deserving of Spirit-empowered praise. We should seek the Spirit's presence and empowerment for our worship of God today, for he dwells near the sincere and humble heart that desires his honor above all.

Knowing God through the Spirit

The Gospel of John especially emphasizes the theme of knowing God personally through the Holy Spirit. The Holy Spirit undoubtedly led John to emphasize this theme because it was so important to his readers, who were mainly Jewish Christians. Leaders of their synagogues had expelled them from the synagogues and sometimes handed them over to hostile Roman authorities because of their faith in Christ. In the ensuing conflict with the synagogue, when local Jewish leaders were appealing to their superior knowledge of Jewish traditions, John encouraged the Christians to appeal to a more essential kind of knowledge: "We know God himself, because the Spirit of his Son lives in us" (compare, for example, 1 John 4:13).

You may remember that many Jewish people felt that the Spirit of prophecy had departed from Israel. From the time of Malachi on, prophecies were rare, and Israel lacked prophets in the authoritative, Old Testament sense. But Jewish people recognized that someday God would pour out his Spirit on his people in a fuller way, as the biblical prophets had promised (Joel 2:28–29). By appealing to their continual experience with the Spirit, the Christians not only appealed to a supernatural empowerment their opponents did not even claim, but they were also declaring that the time of promise had arrived in Jesus of Nazareth. The presence and manifestations of the Spirit constituted the clearest proof that Jesus was the promised deliverer.

John encourages his readers by telling them that their experience marks them out as God's true servants, but he also calls them into a deeper relationship with God by presenting the ideal meaning of that relationship. By listening to John's words of encouragement to his first readers, we can deepen our own sensitivity to the Spirit.

Jesus' Sheep Know His Voice

How do we recognize the Spirit when he speaks to us? Paul tells us plainly that we do not yet know as we are known (1 Cor. 13:12); yet if we are to grow in our relationship with God, we need to begin somewhere in hearing him. John's Gospel teaches that all of us who are born again have a relationship with Jesus already. We have already begun to know God; we simply need to develop the relationship that God has already given us.

Jesus' sheep know him and know his voice (John 10:4–5, 14). They recognize him when he speaks because they are already acquainted with his character. Thus Nathanael, undoubtedly a student of Scripture (1:45–46), recognized the Lord he already served when that Lord confronted him (1:49). Similarly, Mary did not recognize the risen Jesus by his physical appearance (20:14–15), but when he called her by name—as the Good Shepherd promised to do with his sheep (10:3)—she immediately knew who he was (20:16). In the context of Jesus' promise that his sheep would know his voice, a broken man whose need Jesus touched embraced him readily, whereas the arrogant who rejected Jesus showed that they were not his sheep (9:39–10:10).

How can we know God's character well enough to recognize his voice? Countless Bible passages teach us about him—about a God so merciful and patient that human analogies portray him as almost foolishly indulgent (Matt. 18:24–27; Mark 12:6; Luke 15:12).[1] At the same time, Scripture reveals that God's patience does have its limits with those who continue to take his mercy for granted (Exod. 4:24–26; 32:35; Ps. 78:17–31; Hosea 2:8–10; 11:1–7). John teaches us about God's character in a special way: When one of Jesus' disciples failed to recognize that Jesus perfectly revealed the Father's character, Jesus responded, "Anyone who has seen me has seen the Father" (John 14:9 NIV). Indeed, the very prologue of John's Gospel, which introduces his most important theme, makes this point: Jesus is God's "Word" made flesh. We should pause to observe this point in more detail.

All that God revealed of himself in the written Word, God revealed even more fully in his Word made flesh. Jewish people recognized that God had revealed himself in the Scriptures, and the synagogue officials who had expelled John's readers from their assemblies apparently believed that they knew the Scriptures better than the Christians did (compare John 5:39; 9:28–29). But John claims that the same Word of God we confront in the Scriptures has stepped into human history in the person of Jesus of Nazareth. John thus countered the claims of his readers' opponents, who emphasized their own zeal for God's law: those who claim to know God's law but reject Jesus, reject the true message of the Word itself (5:45–47).

By alluding to the Old Testament story of Moses, John shows how Jesus revealed God's character. As the Word, Jesus had always existed alongside the Father (1:1–13), until finally God spoke his Word as flesh (1:14). Then Jesus became one of us, embracing our humanity and our mortality. In so doing, Jesus revealed the Father's "glory, full of grace and truth" (1:14), a fullness of grace and truth that we all receive when we receive Christ (1:16).

By telling us that Jesus' glory was "full of grace and truth," John tells us more about his character than most of us guess. John alludes to the Old Testament story where Moses went up Mount Sinai the second time to receive God's law. God had told Moses that he was angry with his people and did not wish to dwell among them any longer, but that Moses was his friend (Exod. 33:3, 17). "If I am your friend, then I ask only this," Moses requested. "Show me your glory" (Exod. 33:18). God then explained that his full glory would blow Moses away—no one can see God and live—but that he would reveal part of his glory to Moses (Exod. 33:19–23). The LORD then passed before Moses, showing him part of his glory (Exod. 34:5–7). Yet what God showed his servant was not just some cosmic spectacle of fireworks (although fireworks were included); God revealed his character, his heart, to Moses.

As the LORD passed before Moses, he declared, "The LORD, the LORD, abounding in covenantal love and covenantal faithfulness. His anger against sin is so great that he punishes it for three or four generations—but his love is so great that it stretches to the thousandth generation—so much greater is his mercy than his wrath" (Exod. 34:6–7; see also 20:5–6; Deut. 7:9–10). In other words, God's glory was summarized as "full of covenant love and covenant faithfulness," which could be translated from Hebrew to Greek and Greek to English as, "full of grace and truth." "Grace" means God accepting us because that's the way he is, not because of how we are. The Hebrew word for "truth" in this context means God's integrity, his unfailing faithfulness to his character and to the promises he made in his covenant. When God finished his revelation, Moses acted on his deeper understanding of God's character, pleading again for God to forgive Israel and dwell among them (Exod. 34:8–9). And God, being gracious and merciful, agreed (Exod. 34:10).

Some thirteen centuries later, God revealed his Word again, "full of grace and truth." But this time, more than part of God's glory was revealed. This time the Word became flesh, and the grace and truth revealed in him was complete, unlike the partial revelation in the law of Moses (John 1:17). Although no one had seen God at any time, the only-begotten God, who is in the most intimate relationship with the Father, has expounded his character and nature for all the world to see (1:18). What Moses saw in part, the eyewitnesses of Jesus, who could say "we beheld his glory" (1:14), saw in full. This applies not only to those who walked with Jesus on earth but also to those who have come to know his glory subsequently (2 Cor. 3:2–18).

But though we may expect some fireworks when Jesus comes back, there were no fireworks at his first coming. God's Word came in a hidden way, recognized only by those who had developed some acquaintance with God's character beforehand (John 1:47–51). He revealed his glory in various signs, often to only a handful of people (2:11). But the supreme revelation of his gracious and truth-filled glory was the ultimate expression of his full identification with our humanity: God "glorified" Jesus when his enemies "lifted him up" on the cross (12:23–24, 32–33). We crowned our Lord Jesus with thorns and enthroned him "King of the Jews" on a cross, but in his sacrifice, God accounted him Lord of creation and reserved for Jesus the seat at God's own right hand. In the ultimate act of our rebellion, when we shook our fist in God's face and declared our hatred of our creator, God's emissary offered the ultimate demonstration of God's love for us. "For this is how God loved the world: He gave his uniquely special Son, so whoever depends on him will not perish, but share in the life of the world to come" (John 3:16).

God revealed his glory throughout history, but the ultimate expression of his glory—the supreme revelation of his grace and truth—occurred in the cross. Do we want to know God's heart? John declares that we must look at the cross to find it. Paul informs us of this same reality: while we were yet sinners, enemies of God, he proved his love for us by sending Jesus to die for us (Rom. 5:6–8). Now God has poured out his love toward us by the Spirit he has freely given us (Rom. 5:5; see also Eph. 3:16–19)—an experience that in this context means that the Spirit has come into our hearts, pointing to the cross, and assuring us over and over again, "See! I love you! I love you! I love you!" To the abused child, to the abandoned spouse, to the unappreciated, workaholic pastor, to all the other broken people of our world, Jesus declares the heart of God. When we hear the voice of the one who sent his Son not to condemn the world, but rather to save the world from its sin, we truly hear the voice of God's Spirit. Sometimes we can get so caught up in doing God's work that we forget to pause to listen to God's reassurance of love for us, his Spirit reminding us that we are truly his children (Rom. 8:16; 1 John 3:24; 4:13; 5:6–8). But once we have experienced the soothing touch of God's love in prayer, we are only content when walking in loving intimacy with him.

The Spirit and Jesus' Presence

As a young Christian, I spent time among some particularly zealous Christians who felt that we had to "pray through" for an hour before we could earn our way into God's presence. Most of us realize now that we wasted a lot of hours that could have been spent instead in intimate communion with the God we have grown to love. The writer of Hebrews summons us to approach boldly God's throne of grace (Heb. 4:16), and Paul reminds us that Christ has provided us perfect access to God, which we could not have achieved on our own (Rom. 5:2; Eph. 2:18).

John informs us that we can approach God intimately at any time because we are already in his presence (John 14:16–23; 15:1–11). Our relationship with God is too important for us to have earned it; it comes by grace (Phil. 3:9–10). It is true that disobedience can obstruct our relationship with God (John 14:23–24), but Jesus' triumph on the cross was to free us from both the consequences and the power of sin. We overcome temptation by appropriating God's gracious power, not by waiting until our lives are holy enough to have earned his power (Ezek. 36:27). We learn to appreciate God's abiding presence with us in the same way.

After Jesus uses his coming death as the new standard of love that believers should follow (John 13:31–38), he assures his anxious disciples that though he is going away to the Father, he will return to them again (14:3, 18, 23). We often read the next few lines as a promise of his second coming, but although Jesus promises the second coming in other passages, that is probably not what the promise of John 14:1–3 means in context. In this passage, Jesus assures his disciples that he is going away to the Father's house to prepare a place for them among the many dwellings there (14:2; KJV's "mansions" is a mistranslation based on the Latin Vulgate). He promises that he will return to them and that they will be with him forever in his Father's house. How do we know what Jesus was talking about? Even Jesus' original disciples were confused (14:5)! But the context goes on to clarify Jesus' point.

First, Jesus explains what he means by his coming again. In the context, he is speaking of his coming to the disciples after the resurrection (14:16–20; 16:16, 20–22). At that time he would give them his Spirit, through whom they would experience his presence and resurrection life (14:16–17, 19; 20:22). Second, Jesus explains what he means by "dwellings." This noun appears only one other time in the entire New Testament—later in this passage, where Jesus develops the information he has already given his disciples about dwellings. Through the Spirit, Jesus and the Father would come and make their dwelling within each disciple (14:23), thus making them temples of the Lord (the Father's house). The term "dwell," or "abide," which is the verb form of "dwelling," appears repeatedly in John 15, where Jesus dwells with us and we with him (15:4–7, 9–10).

Finally, since Jesus' first disciples did not understand what he was saying either, his explanation to them should prove instructive to us as well. When Jesus noted that they already knew where he was going and how he would get there, one confused disciple protested, "Lord, we do not know where You are going; how can we know the way to get there?" Jesus replied that he was going where the Father was, and Jesus was the way the disciples would get there (14:6; see also 16:28). John 14:6 is talking about salvation; we come to the Father through Jesus. This being the case, we must recognize that Jesus' earlier words in 14:2–3 also speak of a relationship beginning at conversion. When we come to the Father through Jesus, we become his dwelling by the Spirit he has given us. If John 14:6 refers to salvation (and it does), then the question it answers cannot merely refer to the second coming of Jesus that we look for in the future.

God's continuous presence and life-giving empowerment is one aspect of the Spirit's work that rarely appears in Jewish literature contemporary with Jesus. Jewish people spoke of God's purifying his people through his Spirit or empowering some to speak for him through his Spirit. But the early Christians who experienced the Spirit recognized that the Spirit living inside them meant something more; it meant that God himself lived inside them, that they were God's holy temple (1 Cor. 3:16; Eph. 2:22; 1 Peter 2:5; compare the "Father's house" in John 14:2 with John 2:16). Although not to the same degree, this experience already had biblical precedent (Gen. 41:38; Num. 27:18; 1 Peter 1:11; compare Dan. 4:8–9, 18; 5:11, 14; 1 Peter 4:14).

God not only wanted to save us from hell, he wanted to cleanse us from sin; and God not only wanted to deliver us from sin, but once he has purified our house, he wants to live in it with us. Although some other Jewish people, like the writers of the Dead Sea Scrolls, saw their community as a new temple for God, early Christians went beyond this. Viewing each individual believer as a temple as well (1 Cor. 6:19), they recognized that the Spirit dwelt continually in each believer's heart and provided each believer with continual, intimate communion with God (Eph. 3:17–19). It was expedient for us that Jesus go away, so that he could return to be present with each of us in a deeper and more intimate way than before (John 16:7, 12–15). How marvelous is God's great love!

The Spirit Reveals Jesus to Us

Jesus had been telling his disciples that the Spirit would further explain the teachings he had given them—not to make up new things that had little to do with the Jesus they had known (1 John 4:2–6), but to teach them and explain what Jesus had already begun to reveal (John 14:26; compare Neh. 9:20; Ps. 143:10; perhaps Prov. 1:23). In John 16, Jesus explains further how the Spirit would carry on Jesus' mission. (John intends this promise for his readers, not just for Jesus' first hearers [see 1 John 2:20, 27].)

John 16:1–11 encourages persecuted Christians by telling them that those who drag them into court are themselves the ones on trial, because God is the ultimate judge. In God's courtroom, the Spirit is their "Paraclete" (translated variously "comforter," "counselor," "advocate"), a term which often meant a "defense attorney" (1 John 2:1). In the same way, the Spirit testifies along with us as a witness for Christ (John 15:26–27) and prosecutes the world concerning sin, righteousness, and judgment (16:8–11). Everything that Jesus says the Spirit will do in the world, Jesus himself had done (3:18–19; 8:46; 15:22). In other words, the Spirit carries on Jesus' mission of revealing the Father, in a sense mediating Jesus' continuing presence, so that by the Spirit Jesus continues to confront the world as he did personally two thousand years ago. Of course, the Spirit does not reveal Jesus in a vacuum; when Jesus sends the Spirit to convict the world, he sends the Spirit, not directly to the world itself, but to us (16:7, the Spirit is sent "to you," that is, to Jesus' disciples). The Spirit continues to confront the world with the person of Jesus through our proclamation of him.

Just as the Old Testament prophets knew God well before they proclaimed him, our proclamation should flow from a deep and intimate knowledge of God. The Spirit not only empowers us to proclaim Jesus to the world but testifies to us about Jesus for our own relationship with him (16:12–15; see also Eph. 2:18; 3:16). The Spirit will take the things of Jesus and reveal them to us, glorifying Jesus as Jesus himself glorified the Father (John 16:14–15; see also 7:18, 39; 17:4). As soon as he returned to them after the resurrection, Jesus gave his followers the Spirit so that they could continue to know him (16:16; 20:20–22).

Jesus promised that whatever the Spirit would hear, the Spirit would make known to the disciples (16:13). To someone reading the Fourth Gospel from start to finish, this promise would sound strangely familiar. Jesus had just told his disciples, "I have not called you slaves, but friends, because a slave does not know what the master is doing, but whatever I have heard from the Father, I have made known to you" (15:15). Friendship meant many different things to people in the ancient Mediterranean world, but one aspect of friendship about which moralists often wrote was the intimacy that it involved: true friends could share confidential secrets with one another.[2] As God said to his friend Abraham, "Shall I hide from Abraham the thing which I am about to do?" (Gen. 18:17).[3] Moses, too, as God's friend, could hear his voice in a special way (Exod. 33:11; Deut. 34:10). Jesus was open with his disciples about God's heart, and promised that the Spirit would be as open with the disciples after the resurrection as Jesus himself had been before the resurrection. Ancient philosophers emphasized that friends shared all things in common;[4] Jesus explained that all that belonged to the Father was his, and all that was his would be the disciples' (16:14–15). In the context, Jesus especially intended God's truth (16:13). They would know the heart of God.

What does this promise mean for disciples today? It means that the Spirit passes on Jesus' words as clearly as Jesus passed on the Father's, that we should be able to hear Jesus' voice as clearly today as his disciples did two thousand years ago and—since we see things in light of the resurrection—understand his message better. Of course, Christians have often abused the promise of hearing God's voice, hearing instead only what they wanted or expected to hear. What objective guidelines can help us learn sensitivity to the Spirit and enable us to hear God's direction accurately?

First of all, the Spirit does not come to testify about himself; He comes to testify about Jesus (15:26; 16:14). He brings to our remembrance and explains what Jesus has already said (14:26). What the Spirit teaches us is therefore consistent with the character of the biblical Jesus, the Jesus who came in the flesh (1 John 4:2). The more we know about Jesus from the Bible, the more prepared we are to recognize the voice of his Spirit when he speaks to us. Knowing God well enough to recognize what he *would* say on a given topic can often inform us what God *is* saying, because God is always true to his character. But be warned: those who take Scripture out of context thereby render themselves susceptible to hearing God's voice quite wrongly.

Second, the Spirit does not come merely to show us details such as where to find someone's lost property, although the Spirit is surely capable of doing such things and sometimes does them (1 Sam. 9:6–20). Nor does the Spirit come just to teach us which sweater to put on (especially when it is obvious which one matches) or which dessert to take in the cafeteria line, as a few of us charismatics (myself included) in our well-intentioned, spiritually youthful zeal for the details of God's will may have at one time supposed. The Spirit does, however, guide us in evangelism or in encouraging one another (for example, Acts 8:29; 10:19; 11:12.) The Spirit also comes to reveal God's heart to us, and God's heart is defined in this context as love (John 13:34–35; 15:9–14, 17). To walk in Christian love is to know God's heart (1 John 4:7–8; see also Jer. 22:16).

Third, it helps if we have fellowship with others who also are seeking to obey God's Spirit. In the Old Testament, older prophets mentored younger prophets (1 Sam. 19:20; 2 Kings 2:3–8). And among first-generation prophets in the early church, Paul instructed the prophets to evaluate each others' prophecies, to keep themselves and the church on target (1 Cor. 14:29). Spiritual mentors or peers who are mature in their relationship with God and whose present walk with God we can trust can seek God with us and provide us a "safety net" of sorts. If we feel that the Spirit is leading us to do something, but recognize that much is at stake if we are wrong, we may do well to talk the matter over with other mature Christians. Proverbs advised rulers that wisdom rests in a multitude of counselors, and that advice remains valid for us as well. In the end, we may not always settle on the counsel others have given us—like us, they too are fallible—but if they are diligent students of the Scriptures and persons of prayer, we should humbly consider their counsel. God sometimes shows us things for the church that others may not yet see; at the same time, God may well have shown some of our brothers and sisters things we have not yet seen. I have a few spiritual mentors and peers whose counsel I especially treasure and whose wisdom time has consistently (though not always) vindicated.

Many of us as young Christians were intrigued by the frequent experience of supernatural guidance from the Holy Spirit. While most of us who have learned to hear the Spirit in that way still experience such guidance regularly today, after a number of years, sensitivity to the Spirit's guidance in that form becomes almost second nature and thus becomes less of a focus than it once was. Nor is this guidance, exciting as it may be to one discovering it for the first time, always the most important form of guidance God's Spirit gives us. By this method of hearing the Spirit, we might help someone in need, because the Spirit specifically directed us to do so. But many of us have also learned to hear God's Spirit exegetically, as the Spirit has spoken in the Scriptures. By hearing the Spirit's voice in Scripture, we might help that same person in need simply because Scripture commands us to do so. But perhaps the deepest sensitivity to the Spirit comes when we learn to bear the Spirit's fruit in our lives—when our hearts become so full of God's heart that we help that person in need because God's love within us leaves us no alternative. All three forms of guidance derive from the Spirit and from Scripture. Yet where needs clearly exist, God's character that we have discovered by means of Scripture and the Spirit is sufficient to guide us even when we have no other specific leading of the Spirit or scriptural mandate, provided neither the Spirit nor the Bible argues against it. It is when the Spirit has written the Bible's teaching in our heart that we become most truly people of the Spirit.

The Spirit's Leading

Most of all the Spirit leads us into a deeper relationship with Jesus (John 16:13; compare 14:6). But this relationship occurs not only in prayer but in the context of our daily lives. In Romans 8:14, the context evokes the language of the Exodus, when God led his people in the wilderness (Isa. 63:10–14). By this imagery Paul shows that the Spirit brings us into the Christian life and then guides us throughout, ensuring that we will safely enter our future "inheritance" as Israel entered theirs (Rom. 8:15–17). Though we often do not realize it, the Spirit joins us and the rest of creation in "groaning" with birth pangs for the coming age (8:22–23, 26; the Greek term evokes the image of Israel sighing under Egyptian bondage). Similarly, the Spirit often leads us without our realizing it. He takes the struggles of our daily lives and uses them to conform us to Christ's image (8:18, 28–30). In the context of Galatians 5:18, being "led by the Spirit" may also include ethical empowerment—God leading us in the ways of righteousness for his name's sake (Gal. 5:13–6:10; compare Ps. 23:3; 25:4–5, 8–10).

But while these texts present a general leading of the Spirit, other texts indicate that the Spirit clearly can speak and give direction on other matters too. The Spirit not only assures us of our relationship with God (Rom. 8:16) but can guide us concerning specific matters of personal evangelism (Acts 8:29; 10:19; 11:12). To illustrate this point, I offer two more dramatic examples.

One day as I was walking home from the store I felt urged by the Spirit to catch up to the young man in front of me and to call his name (Matt, as I recall). I had never met Matt before; in fact, it turned out that he had just moved to town a few days earlier. Unfortunately, I was afraid to simply call out his name, but when I caught up with him, his name indeed turned out to be Matt. Needless to say, the Lord arranged a profitable time of witness. I felt led to say something about my urban ministry training in New York, even before learning that he had just arrived from there. Often I have felt the Spirit's prompting to witness to a particular person, but he does not usually give me the person's name!

On a much earlier occasion, while I was home from college for the summer, I was translating and studying Romans 8 in preparation for a midweek Bible study I was to lead two days hence. Suddenly I felt the Spirit impress on me that he wanted to demonstrate just how meticulously he can guide us when he wills to do so. Being a budding Bible scholar, I did not really want to interrupt my study, but I thought that I had better obey him if I wanted his help when I stood before the congregation on Wednesday night. The Spirit had sometimes led me like this before, so I knew how to be sensitive to his direction.

After I stepped outside, the Spirit led me up the street, down another street, up another street for some blocks, and finally onto a side street. After I had walked on that street for some distance, the impression left, so I stopped and turned around to get my bearings. As I turned around, I spotted an old friend from high school, and beside him I saw a young woman I had first met on the other side of town three days before and for whose salvation I had since been praying. As I approached, my friend from high school (who was still not a Christian) began telling her how dramatically I had changed after my conversion and was witnessing to her for me. After that, she opened up to me, but she had no permanent address. Sometimes she stayed with various friends and at other times lived on the street. Whenever I needed to reach her, I would just start walking and trust the Holy Spirit to take me to her, as he invariably did. This was not my everyday experience, but I believe that God cared so much about this young woman that he was prepared to use unusual means to show her his concern. (Jesus multiplied food for the five thousand because a miracle was needed; then he had his disciples collect the leftovers because they didn't need another miracle for their *next* meal. He does miracles when we *need* them—not for our entertainment or to make us feel "spiritual.") She had prayed to accept Christ as a child but grew up in a home where, among other things, her mother slept with various boyfriends in front of the children. The young woman was by this time an alcoholic, but Jesus had not forgotten her or stopped reaching out to her.

The Spirit can direct us in a number of ways. Although the Spirit testifies of our relationship with God to our spirits (Rom.

8:16), Paul also speaks of the "mind of the Spirit" (8:5–6) and the "renewing of our minds" (12:2; see also Eph. 4:23; Phil. 4:7–8; Col. 3:2). Proverbs encourages us to seek genuine wisdom based on the fear of God (1:7); such wisdom also provides us with God's guidance. Then too, if we are willing to obey Him, we can trust God to order our steps and situations even when we have no specific guidance. At numerous critical points in my life God has had me cross paths with individuals with whom the chance meeting was a one in a thousand "coincidence," yet that meeting significantly affected the subsequent course of either their life or mine.

Hearing God's Voice: A Personal Account

Although a convinced atheist by age nine, I was converted through the witness of some Baptist street evangelists at the age of fifteen, the first day I heard the gospel. I had argued with them for forty-five minutes, but the Spirit worked me over for the next hour or so until, on the floor of my bedroom, I acquiesced and surrendered my life to him. Over the next couple of years I studied the Bible and led many people to Christ, but I felt frustrated; I wanted to ask God so many questions, but I did not know that he would still speak today. One day as I was walking down a deserted road praying, the Spirit sparked faith in my heart that he would grant the desire of my heart. So I asked him to open my ears to hear his voice. What I heard then was so wonderful that I almost could not believe it, yet it was so far beyond what I could have conceived by myself that I could not doubt it.

I had unconsciously expected God to be like some other authority figures I had known—to say something like, "It's about time you showed up, Keener!" Instead, he said, "My son, I have been waiting so long to tell you how much I love you." And then he began to talk with me about his love for his people and how it broke his heart that we were so wrapped up in all our other pursuits (including many of our religious pursuits) that we did not really understand his love. No one had ever loved me the way God did, and each day I would go out to walk along that same deserted road to listen to the voice of the one who had wooed me to himself. He told me that the measure of his love was the cross: "See the nails in Jesus' hands, the thorns in His brow, and see the blood. My son, that's how much I love you." I later discovered the same teaching in Scripture (Rom. 5:5; 8:16; Gal. 4:6; Eph. 3:16–19), and still later I realized that this teaching was what I had discovered as a seventeen-year-old seeking God's voice. God in his kindness showed it to me when I needed to hear it, before I had learned how to translate Greek and Hebrew and even before I had immersed myself in Scripture in context. Sometimes when we talked, God spoke about impending judgment and other less pleasant topics, but he always did so sorrowfully and always pointed me back to his heart of love.

I began to exercise the gift of prophecy, which was like a new toy to me. I began going to people and prophesying words that answered prayers for wisdom that only they and God knew about. But as I matured, I realized that prophecy was not meant to be a toy; God gave us the gift to show us his heart so we could do his work. Mistakes in finding guidance in my own life slowly persuaded me to take seriously the Bible's claim that all prophecy must be tested and that I remained a finite and fallible vessel.

It was then, through the influence of some godly professors like Benny Aker, that I discovered another method of hearing God's voice that could complement and anchor the "charismatic" method: exegesis, sound Bible interpretation. The Spirit enabled me to see the importance of understanding the Bible in context, and from context I was led to a passion for the Bible's cultural background. Whole new horizons of Bible study began to open to me. I worked hard to set aside my presuppositions and traditions and just go where the biblical evidence led. Those who have read my other books, like *The IVP Bible Background Commentary: New Testament*,[5] may have ascertained this aspect of my devotion to God.

But in 1987, in the deepest crisis of my life, I learned still another way of hearing God's voice, related to the first two. Before that crisis I was praying two hours a day; afterward I could only weakly mutter Jesus' name over and over. Although I was so broken and overwhelmed that I could not hear him at all except on rare occasions, I still clung to what Scripture taught me about God's character.

In the midst of this deepest darkness in my life, some African American Christians in the low-income neighborhood where I had moved unofficially adopted me into their family and took me to church with them. The family consisted of a grandmother and the five grandchildren she was raising by herself. Their own lives were hard, yet they had learned how to draw on God's strength in ways that I had not. As I learned to let go of my ambitions and embrace brokenness, my personal pain began to bond me with others who were in pain. As I grew to feel their pain, I began to realize afresh God's pain—for he loved all people too much not to feel their pain.

John says, "Everyone who loves has been born of God and knows God. Whoever does not love does not know God, because God is love" (1 John 4:7–8 NIV). I will never doubt that God genuinely provided my charismatic and exegetical experiences, but it was in my pain that I learned another way of hearing God to which both the Spirit and Scripture testify. As we begin to know God's character and become like him, we begin to share his heart as well as know about it. When we can not only say what God is saying on some issue, but actually feel what he feels about it, sharing in the fellowship of Christ's sufferings and in the power of his resurrection (compare Phil. 3:10), then we have begun to know him still more deeply.

The Spirit's Fruit (Gal. 5:16–25)

If conversion applies to believers the saving work of Christ, the continuing work of the Spirit causes us to grow in his character. Although God had given his people a good standard for ethics, they had repeatedly broken his covenant. He knew that his people would keep the law only if it were written in their hearts (Deut. 30:11–14). Jeremiah thus promised a new covenant where God would accomplish just that (Jer. 31:31–34). Ezekiel explains how this moral empowerment would work: God would cleanse the spirits of his people and place his own Holy Spirit within them (Ezek. 36:26–27). Paul regularly echoes this promise: the Spirit transforms us to live God's way (Rom. 8:2–10; 14:17; Gal. 5:13–6:10; compare Gal. 2:20 with Gal. 5:24–25; Rom. 15:30; Eph. 4:25–32; Phil. 2:1; Col. 1:8; 1 Thess. 4:8; 2:13; 1 Peter 1:2, 22; 1 John 3:6, 9; 5:18). Old Testament law, like other laws, dealt with people on the outside, but Jesus' coming gave us the Spirit to make us new on the inside so that we would want to do what's right. As Paul points out in Galatians, one cannot be legalistic and walk in the Spirit at the same time. Legalistic religion depends on the flesh; Spirit-filled religion depends on God and the power of his grace.

Not everyone shared Paul's understanding of God's grace in Jesus. Some Jewish Christian "missionaries" in Galatia were trying to impose Jewish customs on Paul's Gentile converts. Throughout Paul's letter to the Galatian Christians, he responds repeatedly that whereas human religion appeals at best to the accomplishments of the "flesh," salvation must depend solely on God's work by the Spirit (Gal. 3:2–5; 5:5, 16–25; 6:7–8), through whom Christ lives in us (2:20). Although Paul gets his contrast between "flesh" and "Spirit" directly from the Old Testament (Gen. 6:3; Isa. 31:3), some of his contemporaries had further developed this idea (especially in the Dead Sea Scrolls): what is "fleshly" is merely human, mortal, and inadequate to stand before God; God's Spirit, by contrast, is the source of true and eternal life.

Paul warns his Galatian readers that love is the true fulfillment of the law (5:13–14), but that "fleshly," human religion leads only to spiritual competition and animosity (5:13, 15). Jewish people often spoke of "walking" according to God's commandments and so fulfilling them. So Paul declares that if we "walk" by the Spirit, we will not fulfill fleshly passions. If one reads Paul's words in the Greek, one discovers that he states the matter in the strongest possible terms: you cannot do the Spirit's will and at the same time do that of the flesh (5:16). Paul then offers the reason for this incompatibility: the goals of the Spirit and the flesh are mutually exclusive (5:17).

Greek philosophers sometimes said that the wise man needed no external law. Here Paul declares that those whom the Spirit leads are not "under the law" (5:18). Paul undoubtedly meant that believers led by the Spirit would fulfill the moral principles of the law, such as love, because the law was written in their hearts (Jer. 31:33; Ezek. 36:27). He contrasts this Spirit-led lifestyle with a life fueled by merely fleshly, human power, no matter how religious it might pretend to be outwardly. He employs the standard ancient literary device of a vice list to show that the "works" of the flesh included all manner of sins (Gal. 5:19–21). Because Paul has been complaining about human "works" in religion throughout his letter to the Galatians, we may be sure that he expects them to see here the inadequacy of human religion.

Instead of dependence on "fleshly works," Paul calls believers to produce the "fruit" of the Spirit. In contrast to fleshly works, particularly hypocritical religion that pretends to be righteous while providing only a thin veneer for sinful passion, Paul recommends something more like what a tree produced by its very nature. Jesus said that one would know a tree by its fruit. Paul, who declares that Christians are new creatures in Christ, expects that our very nature and the presence of God's Spirit within us will of themselves produce good fruit, unless we willfully repress them. For Paul, Christians' behavior should flow from their new identity, and their identity is determined, not by their past, but by their destiny with Christ (Rom. 6:4–5).

Not fleshly works but the transforming power of Christ and his Spirit within the believer produces such works. Those who are in Christ belong not to the flesh, but to the Spirit. Therefore, Paul says, let them live like it (Gal. 5:24–25). Jesus saved us from sin—both its power and its penalty—when by faith we depended on him alone to save us. Paul tells us that in the same way we can now live like we are saved from sin—by faith in Christ's finished work (Gal. 2:20; 5:24; 6:14; by "reckoning ourselves dead," as he puts it in Rom. 6:11). By his Spirit, God has made us new creations in Christ (Gal. 4:29; 6:15). The same Spirit empowers us to recognize our new identity in Christ; one determined not by feelings, not by our past, not by our circumstances, but by the gospel of Christ (Gal. 5:16, 25; see also Rom. 8:13). The Spirit empowers us to live out our identity as God's people recreated in his image (compare Eph. 4:24). Every good work the gospel produces in us is "fruit" (Col. 1:10; Phil. 1:10–11), which comes from understanding how to love (Phil. 1:9) and includes joyful endurance (Col. 1:11) because of our future hope (1:12).

Whereas Paul's Jewish contemporaries stressed the Spirit's work in purification and especially in prophetic empowerment, they included little if any emphasis on continuous ethical empowerment or on sharing God's moral character through the Spirit. Yet this is Paul's point here about the Spirit's work in believers' lives. Paul stresses the fruit of the Spirit, not because many of his contemporaries did so, but because it was part of the reality early Christians experienced in Christ, about which Jesus had informed them (John 15:1–17).

Particular Fruits of the Spirit

Although Paul's list of the fruits the Spirit produces in the believer (Gal. 5:22–23) is probably ad hoc, like his lists of spiritual gifts (see Eph. 5:9; Phil. 1:11; Col. 1:6, 10; compare James 3:17), the sample of fruit he provides can give us a good sense of the kind of life the Spirit produces. Legalistic religion often produces quarrels and spiritual competition; it is self-centered, empowered only by the "flesh," that is, by the self (Gal. 5:13–15). By contrast, the Spirit summons us to self-sacrificial, loving servanthood. The Spirit produces cooperation and wholesome relationships within Christ's body (Gal. 5:25–6:10). His presence and influence in our lives is evident when we begin to act like he does.

LOVE

The fruit Paul lists first is the most important in this context (5:22; see also 5:13–15, 5:26–6:2). Paul elsewhere lists faith, hope, and love as primary Christian virtues (Gal. 5:5–6; 1 Thess. 1:3; Col. 1:4–5), but the greatest is always love (1 Cor. 13:13). For many ancient writers, love was but one virtue among many; early Christian writers, following Jesus' own interpretation of biblical law (Mark 12:29–31; John 13:34–35; 15:12; Rom. 13:8–10), agreed that love was primary.

Love is the fruit Paul most wishes to emphasize here, because it fulfills the moral intention of the whole law (Gal. 5:14; 6:2). The Galatians were concerned to fulfill the law through their own efforts, but throughout the letter Paul insists that if Christ's Spirit lives in them, they will fulfill the law's intention simply by the fruit of love. Instead of legalistic attempts at human moral achievement, they needed to depend in faith on Christ's finished work and to live out that faith by walking in love (Gal. 5:6). Many of the other expressions of the Spirit's presence relate to this fruit of love—for example, peace with one another, patience with one another, meekness (Gal. 5:22–23; 6:1). "Against these," Paul cries, "no law exists!" (5:23; see also 5:18; 6:2).

JOY

Joy is the language of celebration and worship that believers offer because we have confidence that God is with us (Ps. 5:11; 9:14; 13:5; 32:11; 35:27; 42:4; 43:4; 48:2, 11; 63:7; 67:4; 71:23; 105:43; 119:162; 132:9, 16; 149:2). Some Christians accustomed solely to rationally oriented worship services resent the spirit of celebration in many African American, non-Western, and traditional Pentecostal churches. Church services should include a rational component of teaching, and it is possible for emotion to become disorderly, but that Paul puts joy second in his list of the Spirit's fruit should challenge worship that suppresses joy. Our specific ways of expressing joy and praise, whether demonstratively (for example, by dancing, Ps. 30:11; 149:3; 150:4)[6] or more quietly (by being still before God, Ps. 46:10), are often culturally based. But whether quietly or loudly, we should rejoice in the Lord as a sign of our trust in him. In many Black Baptist, Latino Pentecostal, and other churches I know, people struggle in difficult jobs all week long and gather to celebrate the goodness of God in bringing them through another week. I myself tend to worship quietly, but no one has the right, based on one's own idea of how churches should worship, to deny other brothers and sisters the freedom to express their joy demonstratively. If anything, the psalms may support the exuberant forms of worship more than they do the quiet ones, though I believe both have their place. Although trials sometimes make joyous celebration difficult (the psalms are full of mourning as well as joy), under normal circumstances remembering what Christ has done for us should cause us to rejoice (Phil. 4:4–7; 1 Thess. 5:16–18; James 5:13).

PEACE

Peace is the opposite of what the Galatians were experiencing; it is the end of strife (see James 3:14–18). While it might occasionally mean inner tranquility (perhaps in Rom. 8:6), Paul typically uses the term "peace" to mean reconciliation or right relationship with God (Rom. 5:1; compare Eph. 6:15), with one another (Rom. 14:19; Eph. 2:14–15; 4:3; Col. 3:15; 1 Thess. 5:13), and even with outsiders (Rom. 12:18; 1 Cor. 7:15; perhaps 2 Thess. 3:16). Paul regularly regards peace with one another as a fruit of the Spirit. Christians must preserve the unity of the Spirit established among them because God connected them by means of the bond of peace (Eph. 4:3). All his gifts are intended to bring us into deeper unity in the one body and one Spirit (Eph. 4:4–12, and esp. v. 13), a goal that is lived out by loving one another (Eph. 4:25–5:2; 1 Peter 1:22).

Similarly, personality conflict was hurting the Philippian church (Phil. 4:2–3), so Paul presented examples of submission and servanthood: Jesus (2:5–11), Timothy (2:19–24), Epaphroditus (2:25–30), and himself (2:16–18). In this letter he emphasizes unity (1:27–2:4) and notes that God's peace will guard the hearts of his people when they learn to treat one another peaceably and take their needs before God (4:2–9). Although we apply the word "fellowship" glibly today to any conversation between Christians, Paul emphasized the "fellowship of the Spirit" (2:1; see also 2 Cor. 13:14; Acts 2:42–44; 1 John 1:3). As important as customary interpersonal bonding may be, our unity runs deeper than that: the same God lives inside all true Christians, and no one can act like a Christian while despising another member of Christ's body. We cannot help what others do to us, but insofar as it depends on us, we should be at peace with all people (Rom. 12:18). Needless to say, this rules out Christians dividing from one another over issues secondary to the gospel—including different interpretations about spiritual gifts.

LONGSUFFERING

Longsuffering (or patience, or endurance) could refer to enduring any trial (Col. 1:11; James 5:10–11), but Paul usually applies it to relationships. Longsuffering characterizes

God's putting up with humanity (Rom. 2:4; 9:22) and represents how apostles face opposition (2 Cor. 6:1–6). Longsuffering also characterizes how we are to put up with one another (Col. 3:12–13; 1 Thess. 5:14). Paul regularly links this fruit with love (1 Cor. 13:4; 2 Cor. 6:6; Col. 3:12–14) and meekness or humility (Eph. 4:2; Col. 3:12–13).

KINDNESS

In Paul, kindness most often represents God's kindness toward those who don't deserve it (Rom. 2:4; 11:22; Eph. 2:7; Titus 3:4). This is also the way the word is used in Greek versions of the Old Testament (reflecting language Greeks used for benevolent rulers). But kindness can also represent the apostolic model of kindness toward persecutors (2 Cor. 6:6) and the way we should show mercy to one another in Christ's body (Eph. 4:32; Col. 3:12). In Paul's view, such behavior is not natural for people until they have been made new in Christ (Rom. 3:12).

GOODNESS

Goodness characterized the state of obedient believers (Rom. 15:14; 2 Thess. 1:11) and along with righteousness and truth could also serve as a general summary for God's work (spiritual fruit) in our lives (Eph. 5:9; Col. 1:10). Paul borrows the term from the Greek translation of the Old Testament, where it could refer to "good things" materially (Eccl. 4:8; 5:11; 6:6; 9:18), to God's unmerited gift-giving to his people (Neh. 9:25, 35), but also to right moral action (Judg. 8:35 [some manuscripts]; 2 Chron. 24:16), the opposite of wickedness (Ps. 52:3). Paul may apply it as a general term for any moral excellence not covered by his other terms.

FAITH

Faith, or (as many scholars translate it here) faithfulness, refers to the Old Testament idea that one shows trust in God by cleaving to him in obedience based on a relationship with him. Paul often urges such faith(fulness) in opposition to legalistic works in Galatians. We come to Christ and the Spirit by receiving Christ's message in faith, and we continue to grow in faith by the new presence of the Spirit within us (Gal. 3:2–5; 5:5).

MEEKNESS

Meekness represents being unassuming and loving rather than self-centered. It does not necessarily mean being timid, but it means providing the sort of gentle answer that turns away wrath (1 Cor. 4:21; 2 Tim. 2:25; James 1:21; 3:13; 1 Peter 3:15; Prov. 15:1). Paul uses Jesus as his model of meekness (2 Cor. 10:1; compare Matt. 11:29) and expects believers to treat one another the same way (Eph. 4:2; Col. 3:12). Jesus, of course, resisted injustice verbally (Mark 12:38–40; John 18:23) and sometimes even forcefully (Mark 11:15–16), but he did not grasp for human power (Matt. 12:19–20; 21:5). Most relevant to this context, one who exhibits this fruit of the Spirit will show compassion rather than an attitude of condescension to a fellow Christian entrapped in a sin (Gal. 6:1; 1 Cor. 4:21).

SELF-CONTROL

Both in the Greek language in general and in Paul, self-control refers to self-discipline and control over one's appetites— whether sexual (1 Cor. 7:9) or the sort of discipline required when training for athletic competitions, which provides an illustration of Christian discipline (1 Cor. 9:25). Disciplining ourselves to maintain a regular quiet time, to guard our tongue, or to say no to a habit in our lives need not depend solely on human effort (the "flesh"). Whether we recognize it or not, the Christian's success in such endeavors is the fruit of God's Spirit.

Lists of virtues were common in antiquity, and like many of these other lists, Paul's list probably represents merely a sample. Nevertheless, that love stands at the head of Paul's list is no coincidence (compare 1 Cor. 13:13), and we should seek to develop such qualities in our lives (2 Peter 1:4–11). Indeed, they characterize our identity in Christ and show what our life will look like as we submit to the Spirit's gentle leading from within. No spiritual gifts declare us to be people of the Spirit if we do not walk lovingly and meekly toward others.

The Spirit and Submission (Eph. 5:18–21)

Earlier in the book we noted that as important as crisis experiences with the Spirit are, God wants us to be continually full of his Spirit. In Ephesians 5:18, Paul contrasts the kind of inspiration that comes from drunkenness with the kind of inspiration that comes from being filled with the Spirit. The command "Be filled with the Spirit" is followed by a series of subordinate clauses in Greek that are probably intended to provide examples of the life that flows from being Spirit-filled. Moved by the Spirit, believers will worship God with singing and thanksgiving (5:19–20), an experience most of Paul's readers probably took for granted. If charismatic worship occurred in the time of David (1 Chron. 25:1–7), we may be sure that the ideal Christian experience of charismatic worship is even fuller (1 Cor. 14:26; John 4:23–24; Eph. 6:18; Jude 20).[7]

But the Spirit-filled life necessarily includes more than the sort of worship and praise we utter with our lips. It includes "submitting yourselves to one another in reverence for Christ" (Eph. 5:21), which in the Greek text is another subordinate clause explaining what the Spirit-filled life is like. No one who beats his wife or children, spreads slander in a congregation, or harbors perpetual unforgiveness in his or her heart is full of the Spirit, no matter how many supernatural gifts he or she claims to have. Because religious people can embrace all the general principles of Scripture, yet often pretend that most of its corrections do not apply to them, Paul fortunately goes on to describe just what he means by mutual submission.

Writing from a Roman jail cell, Paul was well aware of the crisis facing the early church: the Roman elite who controlled the empire were paranoid about subversive cults undermining traditional Roman family structures and suspected Christians of being among those subversive cults. Paul instructs Christians to uphold the best values of their society, and to do so, he borrows some traditional forms of ethical exhortation. Philosophers from the time of Aristotle on had instructed the male head of the household how to rule his wife, his children, and his slaves. Paul instructs wives to submit to their husbands, minor children to obey their parents, and slaves to obey their masters.

In offering these instructions, Paul nowhere compromised Christian ethics. Christians should submit to those in positions of authority, and the male head of the household always exercised authority over wives, children, and slaves in that society. But while accommodating Roman values where they did not conflict with Christian virtues, Paul recognized that Christian virtues went considerably beyond Roman ethics. Not only those in subordinate positions but also those in positions of authority must humbly serve others. Thus nowhere does he merely repeat the philosophers' traditional exhortation for husbands to rule their wives, children, and slaves.

Instead, Paul expects husbands to love their wives as Christ loved the church and laid down his life for her (Eph. 5:25). In our society, many boys try to become men by making babies instead of raising them, by seeking power over others rather than by using responsibly whatever power they have to serve others, by abusing women instead of respecting, honoring, and serving them. Throughout human history, those who take power are often also taken by it, becoming oppressors of other people. The Spirit's way, however, is different. A Spirit-filled husband must serve his wife even to the point of lovingly laying down his life for her.

In the same way, Paul exhorts fathers not to frustrate their children by unfair discipline. Discipline must always be for the child's good, never a product of the parent's anger (6:4). Finally, after Paul has exhorted household slaves to obey their masters with sincerity, he calls on masters to do the same to them, recognizing that all of us stand the same before God's authority (6:9). If taken to their natural conclusion, such instructions would abolish the abuse of authority, hence abolish slavery itself.

In other words, Paul calls us to honor the authority roles of our culture, if we are in subordinate positions (although he encourages us to improve our situation when possible, 1 Cor. 7:21). If we are in positions of authority, we are to recognize that our authority comes from God and not from anything in ourselves and that our responsibility is to serve. The Spirit-filled life is a life marked by genuine submission to one another. Christians who cannot submit to others, cannot take responsibility, and cannot humble themselves in loving service to others are not yielding to the full life of the Spirit. Christians who gossip, slander, and act arrogantly and with an authoritarian air quench the fruit of God's Spirit. This is true no matter how powerfully these same Christians are able to exercise spiritual gifts and no matter how highly others may rank them in God's kingdom.

The Purpose of Spiritual Gifts (1 Cor. 12–14)

The Corinthian church was like much of the American church today: socially stratified, individualistic, and divisive. Although Paul commends them for their pursuit of spiritual gifts (1 Cor. 1:5, 7), he reproves them for a deficiency far more serious: they lack love, the principle that should guide which gifts they seek (1 Cor. 12–14; 1:10).

Spiritual gifts are for building up the body (1 Cor. 12), and love must coordinate our expression of spiritual gifts (1 Cor. 13). Thus prophecy, a gift that builds up others, is more useful publicly than uninterpreted tongues (1 Cor. 14). Gifts, including prophecy, are no guarantee of spiritual commitment, and one may prophesy falsely or even submit to the Spirit's inspiration without being committed to Christ (Matt. 7:21–23; 1 Sam. 19:20–24).[8] Paul reminds his friends in Corinth that they experienced ecstatic inspiration in Greek religion before their conversion, and points out that the message of Christ, rather than inspiration in general, is what matters (1 Cor. 12:1–3). Communicating the content of God's message, rather than how ecstatically one speaks it, is the important thing. This principle applies not only to tongues-speakers and prophets, but to well-meaning preachers who mistake enthusiasm for anointing while delivering empty speeches devoid of sound scriptural teaching.

Paul then reminds his hearers that all the gifts come from the same Spirit (1 Cor. 12:4–11) and that the gifts are interdependent (12:12–26). Paul ranks the leading gifts (apostles, prophets, and teachers) and then lists other gifts without ranking their importance or authority (12:27–30). Paul urges this church to be zealous for the "best" gifts (that is, those that will best build up the church; 12:31), especially prophecy (14:1). Thus it is appropriate to seek spiritual gifts, but we choose which gifts to seek by determining which gifts will help the body of Christ most. That is, we let love guide our choice (1 Cor. 13).

Paul covers this point in some detail. Even if we had all spiritual gifts in their ultimate intensity, we would be nothing without love (13:1–3). The gifts will ultimately pass away, but love is eternal (13:8–13). While noting the priority of love over spiritual gifts, Paul describes the characteristics of love (13:4–8a). Many of the characteristics he lists (for instance, not being boastful) are precisely the opposite of characteristics he earlier attributed to his readers (see 5:2; 8:1). Thus while the Corinthian Christians were strong in Spirit-led gifts, they were weak in Spirit-led character. For this reason, Paul needed to emphasize the importance of the gift of prophecy, which edifies the whole church, over uninterpreted tongues, which edifies only the speaker (1 Cor. 14). Although Paul focused on what would serve the church as a whole, he was careful not to portray tongues negatively (14:4, 14–19, 39). He exercised this caution even though he could not have known that some later Christians, contrary to 1 Corinthians 14:39, would despise the gift.

The relevance of Paul's words to the Corinthian churches raises the question of whether Paul would have applied the same argument to all churches in his day. As many Pentecostals and charismatics note, some of his specific restrictions on gifts may have applied to the excessive situation in Corinth rather than to all churches. If, as is likely, most Corinthian house-churches seated only forty members, I suspect that the dynamics of spiritual gifts would apply differently there than in a congregation of two thousand members, where more limits would be necessary, or in a prayer meeting of five members, where fewer would be necessary. Likewise, in churches today where spiritual gifts are suspect, prophecy would edify the church no more than tongues would, because even the purest prophecy, approved by other trustworthy prophets, would only introduce division.

Some charismatics insist that the public function of all the gifts, including tongues and prophecy, is so important that we should pursue them (1 Cor. 12:31; 14:1) even if it splits a church. Other charismatics, however, recognize that this view misses Paul's whole point. The purpose of the gifts is to make the body of Christ stronger, and if public use of gifts would divide a non-charismatic congregation, charismatic members should honor the unity of the body first and foremost. This is not to say that they should not work through appropriate channels to bring the congregation to greater biblical maturity in the matter of spiritual gifts. But while gifts are very important and biblical, they are not the most important issue in the body of Christ. The greatest sign of maturity is love.

During the time that a charismatic minister I know was part of a congregation that embraced prophecy, the Holy Spirit moved him nearly every week in the gift of prophecy. When the Spirit led him back to a noncharismatic church, the senior pastor told him that he was welcome to exercise whatever gifts the Lord had given him, including tongues and prophecy. At this church he had more opportunities to minister, especially through weekly teaching from the pulpit. Yet the Spirit never once moved him to prophesy in this church. Instead, the Spirit empowered him in the gift of teaching, which was accepted there.

On occasion, with the full support of the senior pastor, he taught on the Spirit's gifts. But this teaching never became a cause of division. Most weeks he did not address spiritual gifts, however, because there were many other issues that needed to be addressed in the congregation—God's demands for sexual holiness, proper treatment of one's spouse, concern for the poor in the neighborhood, and so on. Teachings on abortion, premarital sex, how husbands should treat their wives, and methods for outreach in the community proved far more controversial than tongues or prophecy. The Spirit continued to move in various ways in this congregation, but while some other issues became mildly divisive, spiritual gifts never did. He never made a secret about his own spiritual experiences, and with the pastor's approval he ministered privately in prophecy when the Spirit would move him to do so while praying with the pastor or other members of the congregation. But some of the friends who ministered to him most deeply there did not share his particular experiences; their unity was rooted in their common fellowship in Christ. Today, although the congregation still has a long way to go, charismatic gifts have begun to flow publicly there without causing any division. Members have offered prophecies on occasion, and the church has embraced the prophecies without a single complaint. This minister and others in the congregation used their charismatic experience to serve Christ's body, not to divide it.

John MacArthur and other critics of charismatic excess are correct in saying that congregations have often divided over spiritual gifts. I have personally witnessed far more cases, however, where mainline churches have been rejuvenated and revived by charismatic evangelical ministers or committed members of the congregation. As long as a congregation acknowledges that spiritual gifts may continue today and does not despise those who exercise or fail to exercise particular gifts, spiritual gifts need never be a divisive issue. That they have often been a divisive issue in the twentieth century is not an argument against their appropriate use. Often those opposed to the gifts have actually created the division, refusing to live at peace with charismatic members. At other times division has arisen from emphasizing spiritual gifts or experiences while neglecting other aspects of the Spirit's work (such as spiritual fruit or sound understanding of the Bible). The division can come from overzealousness or overreaction on either side. But all believers—from the most fervent Pentecostal to the most committed cessationist—can walk in unity if we dare to love one another as Christ loved us. Unity, after all, comes from the one Spirit among us (Eph. 4:3). Many of us believe, however, that the ultimate fruit of this unity will not be the diminution of spiritual gifts, but their restoration to the whole body of Christ, to whom they rightfully belong (1 Cor. 12:12–26).

The Fruits of Pentecost (Acts 2:44–45)

Although the immediate sign of the Spirit's outpouring at Pentecost was a prophetic empowerment for witness, manifested in tongues-speaking (1:8; 2:4, 17–18), the long-range results of Pentecost are the climax of Luke's depiction of the event. The ethnic diversity of those present at Pentecost anticipated the cross-cultural nature of the church (2:9–11) and proved successful (2:41–42). Believers grew in unity around the apostolic teaching and prayer (2:42, 46–47), and apostolic signs and wonders continued (2:43).

Besides the numerical growth of the Christian community, the community grew in its cohesiveness through the believers' commitment to one another. The Greek term for "fellowship" (2:42) could mean economic sharing as well as spending time together. When we go out to dinner with friends from our church after a church service, we often think we are doing well, but the first Christians were far more serious about fellowship in the biblical sense than we are. The believers "shared all things in common" (2:44).

"Sharing all things in common" does not mean that they moved into dormitories or lived on the street together. It does mean that whenever one member of the Christian family had a need, other members sold their possessions to meet that need (2:45). No one claimed that any possessions belonged to themselves; it all belonged to the whole body of Christ (4:32). While we might not trust as many church leaders today to distribute the church's resources equitably (4:35; 6:1–6), the principle remains valid: people matter more than possessions. We should therefore use our resources to meet others' needs (Luke 16:9–15). Our resistance to this unquestionably biblical idea suggests how hard it is for the Spirit to get through our cultural biases.

Luke was not describing a practice he disagreed with. The Greek phrases he uses to describe the church's sharing of possessions portray the ideal community; he presents the early Christians' activity in glowing terms. Despite similarities, the relinquishing of personal property was more voluntary than in Pythagorean or Essene communities (5:4)—it was not "communistic." But by valuing one another more than their property, the Jerusalem Christians showed their concern for God's priorities. This was not a human idea; it was generated by the fellowship of the Holy Spirit. We may contrast today's standard of fellowship, where members often do not even know many others in the church and where single members often leave as lonely as they came.

By collecting money for the saints in Jerusalem (2 Cor. 8–9) Paul applied and expanded this principle of sharing: churches in different parts of the world were helping one another. When Christians in one part of the world are in need today, more affluent parts of the body of Christ must help them. As late as the second century, enemies of Christianity continued to comment how Christians cared for one another by sharing their possessions.

After persecution became rarer and the church began to be able to use its funds for church buildings rather than for caring for the poor or for freeing slaves, the radical commitment of early Christians to care for one another began to wane. Yet this commitment characterized both the first (Acts 2:44–45) and second (Acts 4:34–37) outpourings of the Spirit, and one would expect that it should accompany true outpourings of the Spirit today. Wesley and many other leaders in past outpourings of the Spirit emphasized hard work, thrift, and generosity. Although some who claim to be spokespersons of the Spirit today emphasize how many possessions they can get from God, true people of the Spirit will emphasize how much they can give to serve their brothers and sisters and the cause of Christ.

When we dare to believe Jesus' claims, we will live according to the principle that people matter more than possessions. As a lover of Christ, one cannot accumulate possessions that have no eternal value while people for whom our Lord died go hungry or without the gospel. The issue is not asceticism—as if the lack of possessions makes one more spiritual—but making the needs of others a personal priority. If we really love Christ, we will love others. And this fruit of the Spirit is not just a mushy feeling; it requires action and commitment.

Why Must We Discern the Spirit?

Given my support of spiritual gifts and my own exercise of some gifts like prophecy, I trust that my fellow charismatics will understand that I am not playing down spiritual gifts here. Instead, I am responding to excesses that have often occurred in circles not grounded in Scripture (what some of us have called "charismatic granola"—the "nuts, fruits, and flakes of the Spirit"). J. Lee Grady, editorial director of *Charisma* magazine, authored a book called *What Happened to the Fire?* that every North American charismatic should read.[9] While we each may differ with some of his examples, Grady, as a charismatic, lovingly but thoroughly documents many examples of charismatic flakiness. He shows that sounder self-criticism is needed if charismatics are to contribute to the larger body of Christ with the gifts God has given them.

My criticisms, like Grady's, are made "in-house." I'm attacking not spiritual gifts, but spiritual flakiness. Many anticharismatic complaints about the "bad fruit" of Pentecostal or charismatic doctrine pertain, not to the Spirit or gifts per se, but to the legalism and the opposition to serious Scripture study exhibited by some Pentecostals and charismatics. Often these problems are borrowed from noncharismatic popular religion to begin with. Since some spiritually flaky Christians identify themselves as charismatic, sounder charismatics must take special responsibility to lead others away from such practices. This is what I am seeking to do in this section.

Mature charismatics will concur that not everything that passes as the work of the Spirit among Christians today is in fact from the Spirit. A church's label will not tell you in advance whether the Spirit is present. Contrary to their own claims, for instance, some charismatic churches plainly follow a charismatic tradition by rote; by contrast, in some noncharismatic churches (like the Black Baptist church where I was ordained), only the most spiritually insensitive person could fail to sense the overwhelming presence of God's Spirit. Some charismatics who reject the "tradition" of older churches are similarly bound to more recent traditions based on a "revelation" only a few years old, but it is tradition nonetheless. If we parrot others' teachings without having first checked the context of the passages they quote, we are simply perpetuating tradition, not expounding God's Word faithfully. (In another book I hope to show just how many charismatic proof-texts are really taken out of context.) And if we value our church's tradition more than God's Word, it is our church tradition rather than God that we are serving.

Likewise, not every purported revelation really comes from the Spirit. One questionable revelation occurred while early Pentecostals were deciding the nature of the baptism in the Holy Spirit. Under the Baptistic influence of W. H. Durham, many Pentecostals decided that Spirit baptism was a second rather than a third work of grace. At this time, however, one of the advocates of three stages claimed to have a vision that the devil had instigated the two-stage doctrine to get unsanctified people involved in the Pentecostal movement.

Other "revelations" continued to create problems for early Pentecostal unity. Shortly after much of the Pentecostal movement had settled on two stages, a major segment of the movement split away because one man claimed that one should baptize only in Jesus' name, rendering baptism "in the name of the Father, Son, and Holy Spirit" illegitimate. This "revelation" led to the further view that Jesus was the Father and Spirit as well as the Son—the ancient teaching of Sabellianism, which has little support from the Bible. Many Pentecostals followed the "Jesus only" doctrine, however, lest they dare to question a personal revelation. J. R. Flower, one of the early Assemblies of God leaders, publicly stood against the revelation. Initially he was almost alone in his public declaration that it was unbiblical, but through his courageous stand, most of the Pentecostals who had accepted the revelation returned to the biblical, trinitarian position. Some, however, have continued to teach the Sabellian ("Jesus only") position to this day. It is too easy to blame our bad sermons, bad ideas, and so forth, on the Holy Spirit. Only when we are humble enough to truly learn the difference between the Spirit's wisdom and our own will we press on to spiritual maturity.[10]

Mature charismatics recognize that one must learn Scripture in context, passage by passage and book by book, rather than simply depending on one's own (or someone else's) revelations. As important as our own relationship with the Spirit is, we must maintain a sense of proportion. God's revelations to all his apostles and prophets in the Bible have already been tested; hence the Bible serves as a reliable measuring-stick for all claims to revelation today. Many prophets spoke in Jeremiah's day, but the destruction of Jerusalem revealed that only one of them—Jeremiah—was speaking for God. Jeremiah claimed that the earlier true prophets had prophesied judgment and that this left the burden of proof on any prophet who declared that all would go well with God's people (Jer. 28:8–9; compare 23:16–32). History has tested the biblical revelations, and we must use them to evaluate and guide our own sensitivity to the Spirit. Those who learn to recognize God's voice in the Bible will recognize the Spirit when he speaks in their hearts.

The situation regarding Bible interpretation is more serious than many of us, either charismatic or noncharismatic, realize. Most verses that we randomly quote are quoted by rote rather than by having first studied them in context. Consequently, many of these verses do not mean what we use them to mean. (For instance, the "thief" in the context of John 10:10 is not merely the devil, nor does "lifting Jesus up" in John 12:32–33 refer to praise—as the interested reader may quickly confirm by checking those passages in context.) Sincere, zealous brothers and sisters have too often unquestioningly accepted what popular ministers have said, though some of those ministers quote almost

every single verse they use out of context. Some contend that
God can speak through a Scripture taken out of context. Granted,
God is sovereign and can speak as he pleases—through a proof-
text, a poem, or Balaam's donkey. But we cannot *teach* as authoritative for the rest of Christ's body any interpretation of Scripture that is not genuinely in the text and accessible to all. I do
not mean to attack the ministers who misquote Scripture; if we
pray for them and they have humble hearts before God, God can
lead them to a better understanding. Yet how much better it
would have been to correct the error before they began to mis-
lead so many other people!

We who look the other way while God's servants treat his
Word in ways that we would never let our words be treated must
share the blame. (If someone misrepresented us by quoting us
out of context so severely, we might sue!) I pray for a fresh revival
of the Spirit today—for the awakening of God's church to the
truth of his Word. I recently suggested to another writer, Becky
Groothuis, that maybe the next revival we need is a "hermeneutics movement," where we learn to interpret Scripture in context. Becky jested back that God would not send a move of the
Spirit like that for this dispensation! Yet by God's grace we must
remain committed to fight for it till it comes or we die, whichever
comes first.

I disagree with the conclusion of John MacArthur that miraculous spiritual gifts have ceased, and I am certain that the extreme
examples in his book do not represent most charismatics.[11] Guilt
by association is a specious form of reasoning. For example,
while it is true that cults accept new revelation, most cults accept
new teaching only until the period of their own founding revelation, and they end up denying crucial biblical revelations in
the process—which is not what mainstream charismatics do.[12]
In the same way, if some young charismatics' susceptibility to
false teaching taints the whole charismatic movement, do tainted
charismatics then taint all their fellow evangelicals? In many parts

of the world, most evangelicals are charismatic. Further, main-stream charismatics do not accept new doctrinal revelation that they believe is not in the Bible. Finally, MacArthur himself is not above appealing to postbiblical church tradition, so long as it is not charismatic (that is, if it claims to be true wisdom rather than a true "revelation").[13]

Nevertheless, MacArthur's book does provide useful and accurate examples of charismatic excesses, and unfortunately my fellow charismatics and I could add many more examples that we have witnessed over the years. Some of us recall past fads, such as when some fringe charismatics were having people cough attitude-demons into jars, which would then be sealed and stored in a basement. Once I was going forward for prayer at a church I was visiting when the minister started casting out a "demon of broken wrist" from the lady in front of me. Be assured, I returned to my seat as quickly as possible! I feel more comfortable among anticharismatics who are at least mostly grounded in Scripture than I do among such flaky charismatics.

More to the point—and MacArthur is 100 percent correct on this point—many charismatics (especially in the "faith movement," but also among some noncharismatic pietistic Christians) claim that the Spirit has revealed meanings of Scripture to them when the texts in context have nothing whatsoever to do with their "revelation." If one is going to get revelations that contradict the inspired meaning of the texts one is citing, why not just get the revelations from watching a bird or reading a poem? Why even use the Bible if what it says in context is irrelevant? There is nothing more dangerous than someone acting with the assurance that the Spirit has spoken to him or her when in fact he has not. We should not preach as if the authority of Scripture is behind us, when in fact Scripture in context, apart from our "revelation," does not support what we say. Although most of us know better than to throw out the baby with the bathwater, the bathwater must go. The charismatic early Christians recognized that all claims concerning revelations must be tested (1 Cor. 14:29; 1 Thess. 5:20–22), and they continued in the apostles' teachings (Acts 2:42). It is no wonder that some noncharismatics are afraid that charismatics will go off the deep end. Without careful grounding in Scripture, even well-meaning charismatics, moved by various feelings and predispositions they regard as the Spirit, have often done just that.

Not only is some of what passes for the Spirit not genuine, but some of what is genuinely the Spirit may go unrecognized because of our biases and traditions. Although spiritual gifts and fruits rightfully belong to the whole body of Christ, some charismatics of the separatist variety insist that anyone who believes that spiritual gifts are for today must join their kind of church. Yet as much as some of us enjoy corporate charismatic worship, we believe God's Spirit has led us into, or led us to remain in, Baptist, Methodist, African Methodist Episcopal, African Methodist Episcopal Zion, Lutheran, Catholic, Presbyterian, Anglican, Mennonite, and other churches.

Many charismatics serve as evangelical witnesses in nonevangelical circles. Others remain because the parts of the movements in which they are involved are preaching the gospel soundly, and they feel most at home there. When we minister in these circles, we often find that people are open to our teaching from Scripture, provided that we show the same sensitivity to their church traditions that we would show to any local culture to which the Lord sends us. Conservative and charismatic churches can be dominated by ideologies and personalities that conflict with the gospel just as mainline churches can. Some churches are indeed unfriendly to any words from the Spirit, but this includes some charismatic and Pentecostal churches that have distorted the gospel through legalism or cult figures. Likewise, both noncharismatic and charismatic churches often demonstrate the truth of the gospel and the Spirit's fruit.

While the operation of charismatic gifts in the church is biblical and good, other circumstances being equal, the separatist mentality has serious weaknesses.

First, there are a variety of gifts in Christ's body, some of which are more important for public worship than others. Rare is the church where all the gifts are in full operation, and that includes most charismatic churches. Teaching is a very important gift, yet as we mentioned above and as most sound charismatics will recognize, plenty of unsound charismatics exist. Whether or not one is charismatic, if one regularly studies the Bible in context, one will suffer agony while sitting through a sermon in which the minister rips verses out of context right and left. Although many inadvertently take Scripture out of context and humbly desire God's truth, others arrogantly refuse to admit the need to change, attributing their out-of-context interpretations to the Holy Spirit. The fact that someone has the gift of tongues, prophecy, or healing does not mean that he or she is a good teacher of Scripture. Though I might well speak in tongues more than most of them—to paraphrase a famous charismatic of the past (1 Cor. 14:18)—I would rather serve in a noncharismatic (even anticharismatic) church where the minister usually expounds the biblical text accurately, than a charismatic church that does not do so. Until those charismatic churches who have poor teaching can supply both spiritual empowerment and sound teaching, they will continue to be only a way-station for Christians who need a fresh spiritual experience but who end up taking it elsewhere once they have it.

Second, all the gifts rightly belong to the whole body of Christ. If everyone who privately prays in tongues withdraws into churches that are defined primarily by their public use of particular spiritual gifts, who will remain in noncharismatic churches to introduce others to these gifts in nondivisive ways? Does God call everyone who prays in tongues to worship only in charismatic churches?

Third, all the gifts should build up the body of Christ rather than divide it. Some ministers in the Baptist association in which

I was ordained were concerned about charismatic ministers because a number had pulled their churches out of the Baptist association or had pulled members away from Baptist churches. I think few of our ministers believed that supernatural gifts had ceased; fewer still would have objected to members who personally prayed in tongues or talked about it in a nondivisive way. The fear, however, was division, which does not come from God's Spirit (Rom. 16:17; Jude 19).

Fourth, different churches have different strengths and callings. Ideally, we should be united enough that the strengths of various churches can complement one another. We should be able to learn from and grow in one another's gifts, whether they be teaching, evangelism, or more faith to pray for ailing members in our churches. The pastor of a noncharismatic church in Durham, North Carolina, had a plan to reach the unreached people of that neighborhood, and after weeks of prayer, a young charismatic minister felt that God wanted him to participate in that plan. The Spirit gave this young minister a burden for evangelism that easily took precedence over attending a church where someone could pray in tongues out loud. Although he continued to pray in tongues privately, his public gift involved serving a church that would meet the physical and spiritual needs of that community. Through his presence some others in the church also became more open to various gifts that had not been regularly practiced in that church.

Finally, the common mission that unites us as Christians puts any other particular agenda in second place. Some current issues in evangelicalism undoubtedly are worth dividing over—for instance, whether Jesus is the only way of salvation, an affirmation that I believe is at the heart of the gospel. But most issues we debate among ourselves should not prevent us from working together in our common mission for Christ. Thus, for instance, I may disagree with scholars like Wayne Grudem or J. I. Packer on women's pastoral ministry, yet respect highly their work in other areas like studies on prophecy or knowing God.

I may sharply differ with William Heth's position on remarriage after divorce, but appreciate him as a dear friend; likewise, we both agree that divorce can include an innocent party and that remarried persons should not be excluded from ministry. My views on tongues have little in common with those of John MacArthur, but I appreciate some of his other teachings (I agree, for instance, with lordship salvation). Fortunately, we do not have to repudiate every view someone holds because we disagree on a particular issue. If we broke fellowship with other believers every time we disagreed on some matter, most of us would be left with little Christian fellowship! Charismatic tongues, other spiritual gifts, and beliefs about and experiences in the Spirit may be important, but they do not represent all the issues the Spirit wants us to teach on or the ultimate basis for unity. Even most charismatic churches do not teach these subjects all the time. The Spirit can make a difference in how people look at other issues, but leading people into a deeper relationship with Christ does not mean just teaching them about tongues. It must include teaching people how to understand Scripture, how to carry out Scripture's mandates for evangelism, and how to be sensitive and obedient to God's voice.

Thus we who are charismatics in generally noncharismatic denominations would urge our fellow charismatics not to abandon us without good reason. We need your zeal for the dynamic of God's Spirit among us. And we trust that you will remember that you, too, need other true Christians' gifts, even if some of those gifts seem less spectacular. As Christians, each of us must humble ourselves before all our brothers and sisters in Christ's body (1 Peter 5:5), recognizing the diversity of gifts God has given (Rom. 12:4–8; 1 Cor. 12:14–26; 1 Peter 4:10). Thus we should seek those gifts which will build up Christ's church as a whole and neither despise nor blow out of proportion the role of particular gifts. The ideal, of course, is for all churches, both traditionally charismatic and traditionally noncharismatic, to act fully biblically on spiritual gifts and in every other way. But only if we pursue the fruit of the Spirit now—including love, peace, kindness, and longsuffering—can we hope to achieve that goal. If one had to choose between an emphasis on gifts or on fruit, 1 Corinthians 13 makes clear what our priority should be.

Conclusion

We must seek to cultivate especially those gifts that most build up the body of Christ. We must accept and encourage one another's gifts, and in our pursuit of gifts, honor the unity of Christ's body. The gifts should not be segregated into "charismatic" parts of the church; they belong to the whole body of Christ, a reality that many believers, both charismatic and non-charismatic, have often failed to appreciate.

Yet the "bottom line" of the Spirit's work in our lives is not power to perform miracles, but a transformed heart that learns how to love. Spiritual power without love is dangerous, but love without some degree of spiritual power to carry forth its designs is impotent. Once our hearts are attuned to God's heart in love, we can seek various spiritual gifts for his glory, for serving our brothers and sisters in Christ, and for changing the world around us that desperately needs transformation by Christ's power. We can pray together for the establishment of God's kingdom rather than our own kingdoms. May the Spirit produce in us his fruits, the image of Christ's character, so that the world around us may begin to know what God's love for them looks like. After washing the disciples' feet, as Jesus was getting ready to go to the cross, he commanded them (and us):

> I am giving you a new commandment—that you love one another. You must love one another in the very same way that I have loved you. This is how everyone will know that you are my disciples: if you love one another (John 13:34–35).

Conclusion

I n the broad sense of the term "charismatic," the Bible advocates a position that is more charismatic than the practice of many charismatic churches. Tongues is an important but small part of what the Spirit must do among us today. We also need God's empowerment for deeper intimacy with him, for evangelism, for apologetics, for teaching, for confirming signs like healing, for strength in the midst of testing, for wise strategies to effectively reach our culture and other cultures, and more.

Thus it is possible to affirm that all the gifts are for today, yet to be a cessationist in practice by avoiding the gifts. It is also possible to practice some of those gifts, yet deny in practice what cessationists themselves would not deny—namely, that God also empowers us for daily prayer, evangelism, and holy living. Although we are complete in Christ, our proper attitude in daily prayer may best be summed up by the exclamation of an eager new convert, a state university undergraduate with whom I had lunch: "I can't get enough of Jesus!" Some writers accurately summarize Paul's teaching on our position in Christ as, "Be what you are." We need to appropriate in daily practice all that God has provided us in Christ.

In this book we have asked three crucial questions about the Holy Spirit. First we asked, "What is the baptism in the Holy

181

Spirit?" We concluded that it applies to the whole sphere of the Spirit's work in our lives, so different passages can use the expression in different ways. It can apply both to conversion (where we receive full access to Christ's power) and to an experience of empowerment to speak for God, especially (in Acts) for witness. Second, we asked, "How important are spiritual gifts today?" We recognized that spiritual gifts are intended to benefit the whole body of Christ and that all Christians should view their God-given roles as gifts to Christ's body. There is no biblical reason to assume that any of the gifts should have passed away. Finally, we asked, "How can we recognize the Spirit?" Here we learned that the Spirit has the same nature that Jesus does and that whatever the Bible tells us about Jesus' character applies to the Spirit's character as well. In the same way, our lives should reflect God's moral character in the fruit of the Spirit, who lives within each Christian.

Each of these questions has practical implications for today's church. The practical implications of chapter 1 are that we need to depend on the power of God's Spirit to carry out the task of world evangelization God has given us. If we are converted but lack the requisite power, it is not because God has not provided the power; we must therefore seek him for it. The practical implications of chapter 2 are that we will fall short of accomplishing God's purposes in the world as long as we minimize any of the gifts. Further, God gives us the gifts to build up the body, so debating spiritual gifts in an unloving way is counterproductive to the very purpose for which he gives them. Yet the practical implications of chapter 3 may be the most daunting of all. Through the Spirit, our relationship with the Lord can grow in intimacy, and we can learn to recognize and demonstrate the fruit of the Spirit's presence among us. It is ultimately behaving self-sacrificially as Jesus behaved, not how many spiritual experiences we have, that proves that we are his disciples (John 13:34–35; 1 John 2:3–6). The conclusions for the book as a whole are that the Bible summons all Christians to accept the Spirit's empowerment for the various tasks he has assigned us and for evangelizing the world. Woe to us if in a world like today's we try to do his work without him!

Although I believe that my conclusions flow directly from Scripture, few writers on the issue lack presuppositions. I have learned some of the biblical lessons in this book from other parts of Christ's body, sometimes the hard way. I also admit that despite my best efforts to study the text objectively, my background— both its charismatic and its noncharismatic elements—has inevitably affected the way I approach these questions. Thus my enjoyment of charismatic gifts; irritation at the ways some charismatics have handled Scripture over the years; and my theological home in mainstream evangelical, Baptist, and African American theological circles all affect what issues I think are most important for a book like this one. I trust that readers will take all these factors into account, yet will consider the arguments in this book on their own merits and examine the Scriptures afresh on the issues considered here. I too have more to learn from other Christians who are submitted to Scripture and seeking the Spirit's empowerment.

The fact that my charismatic experience has been part of my Christian life from the beginning—whereas the joys of contextual study of the Bible, concern for the poor in my community, and other experiences came later—may explain why I see this experience as one important experience among many, not as the sole defining experience of my Christian life. Some others, transformed by a dynamic spiritual experience later in life, may see it differently. In either case, however, I believe Scripture is clear that faith in Christ makes us all members of Christ's body. Mature charismatics are those who have depended on the Spirit through hardship and have learned to serve Christ's whole body; charismatics who look down on other Christian brothers and sisters because their spiritual experience is different are immature, baby charismatics no matter how long they have been charismatic. The world may be full of baby charismatics (and baby anticharismatics as well), but God's goal is our maturity in Christ (Col. 1:28). The one Spirit who makes us one body summons us to serve the one body and to evangelize the world together. If we cannot do that, then in practice both our charismatic and noncharismatic claims to having the Spirit are worthless. May all of us live like the people of the Spirit that Christ has summoned us to be—the many-gifted, fruitful body of Christ.

Appendix

What Can Bible Stories Teach Us?

lthough few of our conclusions have rested on narrative alone, some scholars may feel uncomfortable with the way we have used narratives from Acts and elsewhere as models for today, even when those narratives portrayed the perfect activity of God rather than the fallible behavior of his followers. Because others have already written so much on Paul's treatment of the Spirit,[1] in this book I often emphasized the narrative portions of the New Testament—that is, the New Testament stories. Stories can be true stories (like biblical history or biography) or fictitious stories (like parables), and we read history and parables somewhat differently. But both kinds of stories share some common narrative devices, such as a plot and characterization; and in some respects we approach them in the same way. When we read any kind of biblical story, we look for its moral.

This approach becomes especially clear when we compare the differences between Gospels or the overlapping material in Kings and Chronicles. Because Jesus did and taught so much, no one Gospel writer could have told us everything about him (as John 21:25 explicitly points out). Rather, each Gospel writer emphasized certain points about Jesus, the way we do today when we read or preach from a text in the Bible. This means that when we read Bible stories, we not only learn the historical facts about what happened, but we listen to the inspired writer's perspective on what happened—that is, the lessons to be drawn from the story. When the writer "preaches" to us from the stories he tells us, he often gives us clues for recognizing the lessons. For example, a Gospel writer often selected stories with the same basic theme or themes that repeatedly emphasized particular lessons.

Many evangelical restoration movements (for example, German Pietists, Moravians, Wesley's first followers) have looked to Acts for appropriate patterns for church life. Similarly, Baptists (including myself) base our case for believers' baptism by immersion on historical precedent in the New Testament, arguing from what baptism meant in first-century Palestine. (Admittedly, we do not practice baptism exactly the way they did it back then. Formal Jewish baptism rituals were performed nude, and those being baptized probably immersed themselves face forward. Undoubtedly John's public baptisms in the Jordan were done a little differently.) Many churches even base practices on precedents in church history after the completion of the Bible.

Despite such historical precedent, many evangelical scholars today seem nervous about getting theology from narrative (Bible stories). Although few would dismiss the doctrinal value of narrative altogether, many suggest that one should find in narrative only what is plainly taught in "clearer," more "didactic" portions of Scripture. Although some of these scholars are among the ablest exegetes in other portions of Scripture, I must protest that their approach to Bible stories violates the most basic rules for biblical interpretation and in practice jeopardizes the doctrine of biblical inspiration. Did not Paul say that *all* Scripture was inspired and therefore useful for "doctrine," or teaching (2 Tim. 3:16)? I freely admit that I myself do not understand some portions of Scripture—for example, the eternal significance of the genealogies in Chronicles. But other obscure parts began to make sense to me after I understood the cultural context they addressed (for instance, the design of the tabernacle in Exodus). Specific examples of how God worked in narrative often provide only principles rather than promises: for instance, that Jesus healed a leper shows God's power and Christ's compassion, but need not guarantee the healing of all lepers under all circumstances. Some texts are more useful for addressing situations today than others, but all biblical texts have some purpose.

One of the most basic principles of Bible interpretation is to ask what the writer wanted to convey to his contemporary audience. This principle applies to narratives like the Gospels as much as to epistles like Romans. If one could simply write a "neutral" Gospel that addressed all situations universally, the Bible would undoubtedly have included it. Instead, the Bible offers us four Gospels, each one selecting some different elements of Jesus' life and teachings to preach Jesus to the needs of readers in relevant ways. This also provides us with a model for how to preach Jesus in relevant ways to our hearers. The way God chose to give us the Bible is more important than the way we *wish* he would have given it to us.

Further, we must learn to read each book first of all as a self-contained unit, because that was how God originally inspired these books. Books like Mark or Ephesians were written one at a time by authors addressing specific situations. The first readers of Mark could not refer to Ephesians or John to figure out an obscure point in Mark; they had to read and reread Mark as a whole until they grasped the meaning of each passage. When we read a book of the Bible, we need to read each passage in light of the total message and argument of the book as well as reading the book in light of the passages that make it up.

This is not to say that we cannot compare the results from our study of Ephesians with the results from our study of Mark. But we miss the complete character of Mark when we resort to Ephesians before we have finished our examination of Mark. For instance, the opposition Jesus faces for healing a paralytic provides a lesson for the hostility we can expect from the world for doing God's will. The opposition to Jesus that builds in early chapters of Mark and climaxes in the cross parallels the suffering believers themselves are told to expect (8:31–38; 10:33–45; 13:9–13; 14:21–51). Mark summons Christians to endure and provides negative examples of this principle (for example, 14:31–51) as well as positive ones to reinforce his point. Such examples also show Christians' inability to fulfill this call in their own strength.

Most cultures in the world teach lessons through stories. Westerners are the ones who are odd in finding themselves unable to follow the point of narratives in the Bible. In fact, not even all Western Christians find Bible stories inaccessible. Black churches in the United States have for generations specialized in narrative preaching. In most churches, children grow up loving Bible stories, until they become adults and are taught that they must now think abstractly rather than learn from concrete illustrations. That our traditional method of extracting doctrine from Scripture does not work well on narrative does not mean that Bible stories do not send some clear messages. Instead it suggests that the way we apply our traditional method of interpretation is inadequate because we are ignoring too much of God's Word.

When Jesus' followers were writing the New Testament, everyone understood that narrative conveyed moral principles. Ancient biographers and historians expected readers to draw lessons from their examples, whether positive or negative. Students regularly recited such stories in elementary school exercises, and in more advanced levels of education, they learned how to apply these examples to drive home moral points.

Using only nonnarrative portions of the Bible to interpret narrative is not only disrespectful to the narrative portions, it also implies a misguided way of reading nonnarrative portions of Scripture. Everyone acknowledges, for instance, that Paul's letters are "occasional" documents—that is, they address specific occasions or situations. Thus, had the Lord's Supper not been a matter of controversy in Corinth, we would know little about it except from Matthew, Mark, and Luke. If we then were to interpret the narrative portions of Scripture only by other portions, we might assume that we do not need to observe the Lord's Supper today. Of course, Jesus teaches his disciples about the Lord's Supper within the narrative. But since the teaching is within the narrative, we can always protest that he addressed this teaching only to a select group of disciples. A few hundred years ago Protestants explained away the Great Commission in just such a manner. Today many similarly explain away teachings found in the Gospels and Acts about the usefulness of signs and wonders for evangelism.

Not only is the traditional "doctrinal" approach inadequate for interpreting the Gospels, but it is inappropriate for interpreting the Epistles as well. The "narrative" way of interpreting Bible stories in fact helps show us how to read the Epistles properly. Paul never wrote just to say hello; he wrote to address specific needs of churches. While the principles Paul employs are eternal and apply to a variety of situations, Paul expresses those principles concretely to grapple with specific situations. Before we can catch his principles, we often must understand the situations with which he is grappling. Paul's concrete words to real situations are case studies that show us how to address analogous situations today. Paul's letters presuppose a sort of background story—he is responding to events and situations that arose among his original audience. In other words, we must read even Paul's letters as examples. This is how Paul read the Old Testament—drawing theology (especially moral teaching) from its examples (1 Cor. 10:11). Saying that narratives have teaching value does not solve the problem of determining what they teach, of course, as evangelical scholars like J. Ramsey Michaels, D. A. Carson, and Gordon Fee have rightly pointed out when addressing the tongues issue. But students of the Bible must examine the narratives in the Bible as thoroughly as any other part of the Bible, for the teaching God chose to provide there is no less important than what he offered elsewhere in Scripture. That many of the examples in Acts show patterns of *God's* action suggests that these models remain valid for understanding how God has chosen to work (in contrast to examples more bound to the cultures of their day).

I suspect that many scholars—including myself in earlier years—feel uncomfortable finding theology in narrative largely because of their academic training. In the theological academy, one can feel content addressing important issues like Christology while ignoring equally necessary personal issues like domestic abuse and how to witness at work. But pastors, door-to-door witnessers, and other ministers cannot ignore issues that exceed the bounds of traditional doctrinal categories. We should not forget that those general doctrinal categories were established by medieval theologians who often could afford to withdraw from the daily issues with which most of their contemporaries struggled. The issues they addressed were important, but they were hardly exhaustive. I believe that the more we are forced to grapple with the same kinds of situations the writers of Scripture had to face, the more sensitively we will interpret the texts they wrote. When that happens, we will need to reappropriate all of Scripture—including its stories—for the life and faith of the church.

Notes

Author's Preface

1. To keep documentation in the book to a minimum I have cited only sources that address issues (especially regarding church history) quite different from those addressed in my more scholarly work on biblical pneumatology (*The Spirit in the Gospels and Acts* [Peabody, Mass.: Hendrickson, 1996]) due out roughly simultaneously with this work. Readers who wish further documentation on exegetical matters may find it there. I have also focused the documentation on the first two chapters, which address the more controversial topics. For more documentation, one should also consult D. A. Carson, *Showing the Spirit: A Theological Exposition of 1 Corinthians 12–14* (Grand Rapids: Baker, 1987), and Gordon D. Fee, *God's Empowering Presence: The Holy Spirit in the Letters of Paul* (Peabody, Mass.: Hendrickson, 1994).

Chapter 1: What Is the "Baptism in the Holy Spirit"?

1. Craig Keener, "Spirit at Work," *Discipleship Journal*, Jan./Feb. 1996, 43; see full article 43–47.

2. For Wesleyan, Anglican, and Catholic views of the second experience, see W. J. Hollenweger, *The Pentecostals* (Peabody, Mass.: Hendrickson, 1988), 21, 26 n. 2; see at greater length H. I. Lederle, *Treasures Old and New: Interpretations of "Spirit-Baptism" in the Charismatic Renewal Movement* (Peabody, Mass.: Hendrickson, 1988), who provides a full survey of views; Vinson Synan, *The Holiness-Pentecostal Movement in the United States* (Grand Rapids: Eerdmans, 1971), 18–21; and for the most thorough treatment of the terminology's Wesleyan and Holiness roots, see Donald W. Dayton, *Theological Roots of Pentecostalism* (Metuchen, N.J.: Scarecrow; reprint, Peabody, Mass.: Hendrickson, 1994); elsewhere see, for example, John L. Gresham, Jr., *Charles G. Finney's Doctrine of the Baptism of the Holy Spirit* (Peabody, Mass.: Hendrickson, 1987). Some Reformed ministers like R. A. Torrey, superintendent of Moody Bible Institute, Baptists like A. J. Gordon, and others also emphasized the baptism in the Spirit as a second work of grace (Gary B. McGee, "Early Pentecostal Hermeneutics: Tongues as Evidence in the Book of Acts," in *Initial Evidence: Historical and Biblical Perspectives on the Pentecostal Doctrine of Spirit Baptism,* ed. Gary B. McGee [Peabody, Mass.: Hen-

drickson, 1991], 96–118, esp. 101); Richard Baxter and other Puritan and Reformed sealers also envisioned a subsequent work (Lederle, *Treasures,* 5; Dayton, *Theological Roots,* 37). See also Frederick Dale Bruner, *A Theology of the Holy Spirit: The Pentecostal Experience and the New Testament Witness* (Grand Rapids: Eerdmans, 1970), 76, 323–41, who disagrees with subsequence but documents the subsequence positions of Wesley, Finney, Torrey, Andrew Murray, A. J. Gordon, and F. B. Meyer. Many early prejudices against Pentecostalism arose from class and race tensions (Pentecostalism originally appealed especially to the lower class).

3. For a much more detailed treatment of early Jewish understandings of the Spirit (and points below like the antiquity of Jewish proselyte baptism), see the extensive first chapter and relevant points in subsequent chapters of my recent work on early Jewish and Christian views of the Spirit: *The Spirit in the Gospels and Acts* (Peabody, Mass.: Hendrickson, 1996).

4. Matthew adds that those who revile the Spirit's testimony to Jesus (Matt. 12:24, 31–32) thereby reject Jesus' Messianic identity (see Matt. 12:18, 28). Other writers also emphasize how the Spirit empowered Jesus both to perform signs (Acts 10:38) and to suffer (Heb. 9:14). The Spirit is also central in the act of resurrection (Rom. 8:11; 1 Peter 3:18; compare also Rev. 11:11).

5. On the connection between Luke's Jesus and the Spirit-baptized community of Acts, see Roger Stronstad, *The Charismatic Theology of Saint Luke* (Peabody, Mass.: Hendrickson, 1984), 34–48, and 51 (following Talbert); R. L. Brawley, *Luke-Acts and the Jews,* Society of Biblical Literature Monograph Series 33 (Atlanta: Scholars Press, 1987), 24–25; R. F. Zehnle, *Peter's Pentecost Discourse,* Society of Biblical Literature Monograph Series 15 (Nashville: Abingdon, 1971), 128. On Luke's emphasis on the prophetic empowerment dimension of the Spirit, see especially R. P. Menzies, *The Development of Early Christian Pneumatology with Special Reference to Luke-Acts*, Journal for the Study of the New Testament Supplement 54 (Sheffield: Sheffield Academic Press, 1991).

6. Baptism "in Jesus' name" in Acts always occurs only with the passive voice— *receiving* baptism in Jesus' name. That is, contrary to the antitrinitarian interpretation, baptism "in Jesus' name" concerns one's own profession of faith in Christ, not a formula someone else pronounces over one during baptism (see Acts 22:16).

7. On the parallels among figures in Luke-Acts, see especially M. D. Goulder, *Type and History in Acts* (London: SPCK, 1964); Charles H. Talbert, *Literary Patterns, Theological Themes, and the Genre of Luke-Acts,* Society of Biblical Literature Monograph Series 20 (Missoula, Mont.: Scholars Press, 1974); and Robert C. Tannehill, *The Narrative Unity of Luke-Acts: A Literary Interpretation,* vol. 1, *The Gospel according to Luke* (Philadelphia: Fortress, 1986); vol. 2, *The Acts of the Apostles* (Minneapolis: Fortress, 1990).

8. In many parts of the world, the church, less shaped by Western rationalism, already views Christian apologetics especially in terms of power encounter; see, for example, the African perspectives summarized in William A. Dyrness, ed., *Emerging Voices in Global Christian Theology* (Grand Rapids: Zondervan, 1994), 11–12. In the Bible see Exod. 7:8–13; 12:12; 1 Kings 18:20–40.

9. See Gordon D. Fee, *God's Empowering Presence: The Holy Spirit in the Letters of Paul* (Peabody, Mass.: Hendrickson, 1994) and his lexical arguments on this passage. His case is not likely the result of mere presuppositions; Fee rightly disavows most proposed "second work" readings of Paul. He believes that both Paul and Luke show

"that the gift of the Spirit was not some sort of adjunct to the Christian experience, nor was it some kind of second and more significant part of Christian experience. It was rather the chief element of the Christian life from beginning to end" (*Gospel and Spirit: Issues in New Testament Hermeneutics* [Peabody, Mass.: Hendrickson, 1991], 98).

10. Luke explicitly employs the *expression* "baptized in the Holy Spirit" in only two instances: with reference to Pentecost (Acts 1:5; compare 2:1–4) and in Peter's description of the conversion of Cornelius's household (Acts 11:15–16; compare 10:44–47). Good friends of mine therefore argue that the expression applies only to conversion. Although I remain inclined to apply the expression to the whole sphere of the Spirit's work and to think that Luke focuses on a particular aspect of that work that is not always simultaneous with conversion, my *primary* interest in this chapter is the experience and its effects, rather than the precise terminology. Where I am sure that I am correct, and hope my readers will agree, is that Luke shows us that subsequent empowerments, or giftings, of the Holy Spirit are desirable. All the Spirit's power becomes available at conversion, but whereas Christians sometimes experience the full impact of this empowerment at conversion, I believe Acts indicates that this is not always the case. Luke emphasizes this special empowerment for crossing cultural boundaries and evangelizing the world.

11. For an argument that these "disciples" were already Christians, based in part on the grammar of Paul's question, see Stanley M. Horton, *What the Bible Says about the Holy Spirit* (Springfield, Mo.: Gospel Publishing House, 1976), 159–62. Although Horton's book offers many good points throughout, many exceptions make an argument from grammar tenuous here either in support of or against his position.

12. Bruner, *Theology of Holy Spirit*, 177–78, carefully surveys Pentecostal writers (although many Pentecostals today would differ from many of the older positions summarized) and provides a serious analysis of New Testament texts from a charitable noncharismatic perspective. He argues that the delay in Samaria was abnormal and that the Spirit here completes the experience of Christian baptism. If the text implies that the experience was abnormally delayed, we still must ask whether the sort of event depicted here is possible without an experiential dimension; if not, then conversion should normally include a dramatic experience of the Spirit, one that is sometimes delayed (probably more often today than then). This would fit the view of some charismatics who view Spirit baptism as the completion of salvation (in contrast to my view above, that it represents a different kind of empowerment of the Spirit).

13. James D. G. Dunn, *Baptism in the Holy Spirit: A Re-examination of the New Testament Teaching on the Gift of the Spirit in Relation to Pentecostalism Today* (Philadelphia: Westminster; London: SCM, 1970), addresses Acts 8 on pages 55–72. Acts 8 is certainly not a *normative* pattern—God may have allowed the delay to heal the Jewish-Samaritan schism (so Michael Green, *I Believe in the Holy Spirit,* 2d rev. ed. [Grand Rapids: Eerdmans, 1989], 167–68; D. A. Carson, *Showing the Spirit: A Theological Exposition of 1 Corinthians 12–14* [Grand Rapids: Baker, 1987], 144–45). But it does illustrate that God could allow delay; and if he allowed it then, he could also allow it (for different reasons and under other circumstances) today.

14. Dunn, *Baptism in the Holy Spirit,* 55.

15. Clark Pinnock, foreword to *The Charismatic Theology of Saint Luke,* by Roger Stronstad (Peabody, Mass.: Hendrickson, 1984), vii.

16. Dunn, *Baptism in the Holy Spirit,* 55–72.

17. On many of these points, see Howard M. Ervin, *Conversion-Initiation and the Baptism in the Holy Spirit* (Peabody, Mass.: Hendrickson, 1984), 28–32. Although I often agree with Dunn against Ervin, I believe that Ervin has the exegetical upper hand in Acts 8.

18. Fee, *Gospel and Spirit,* 96–99, 117–19.

19. As Carson says, "Although I find no biblical support for a second-blessing theology, I do find support for a second-, third-, fourth-, or fifth-blessing theology" (*Showing the Spirit,* 160). Perhaps one may lose count!

20. Carson, *Showing the Spirit,* 50 (compare also 186).

21. Dallas: Word, 1994.

22. I am heartened to find that others have articulated positions similar to the one I suggest here. See, for example, Lederle, *Treasures*, 151 (summarizing David Watson): all Christians have the Spirit, but not all are filled with the Spirit—the phrase "baptism in the Spirit" including either one—and the power and reality matter more than the terminology anyway. From Lederle's critique of J. Rodman Williams (93–94), I suspect that Lederle would not agree with my views here. The matter requires some charity, since it is more difficult than we would like for any exegete to harmonize convincingly the exegesis of various passages when one has finished with one's own exegesis of each one.

23. James D. G. Dunn, *Jesus and the Spirit: A Study of the Religious and Charismatic Experience of Jesus and the First Christians as Reflected in the New Testament* (London: SCM, 1975), 189–91.

24. McGee, "Hermeneutics," 108–10. For dissent among early Pentecostals, see McGee, "Hermeneutics," 107, and H. I. Lederle, "Initial Evidence and the Charismatic Movement: An Ecumenical Appraisal," in *Initial Evidence: Historical and Biblical Perspectives on the Pentecostal Doctrine of Spirit Baptism,* ed. Gary B. McGee (Peabody, Mass.: Hendrickson, 1991), 131–32. Lederle, *Treasures*, 29–31, also summarizes early Pentecostal theologians who held other views, noting that doctrinal freedom on major issues secondary to the gospel characterized early Pentecostalism (see esp. 29; see also Hollenweger, *Pentecostals,* 32, 331–36). In "Evidence and Movement," 136, Lederle claims that only 35 percent of all Pentecostals have prayed in tongues. For a well-crafted exegetical defense of the classical Pentecostal position, see Donald A. Johns, "Some New Directions in the Hermeneutics of Classical Pentecostalism's Doctrine of Initial Evidence," in *Initial Evidence*, 145–67. Historically the nineteenth-century Catholic Apostolic Church, whose last apostle died the year the modern Pentecostal movement was born (1901), viewed tongues as a prominent sign of Spirit baptism (see David W. Dorries, "Edward Irving and the 'Standing Sign' of Spirit Baptism," in *Initial Evidence*, 41–56; compare Gordon Strachan, *The Pentecostal Theology of Edward Irving* [Peabody, Mass.: Hendrickson, 1973]; Larry Christenson, *A Message to the Charismatic Movement* [Minneapolis: Bethany Fellowship, 1972]).

25. See Cecil M. Robeck, Jr., "William J. Seymour and 'the Bible Evidence,'" in *Initial Evidence*, 81–89; Synan, *Holiness-Pentecostal Movement,* 180. Some of Parham's original ideas concerning tongues, such as that it was xenoglossa or that only tongues-speakers would experience a pretribulational rapture (see James R. Goff, Jr., "Initial Tongues in the Theology of Charles Fox Parham," in *Initial Evidence*, 64–65, 67), were quickly rejected by other Pentecostals, as was his advocacy of British Israelit-

ism. For the usual breaking *down* of racial barriers in early Pentecostal circles, conflicting with broader societal prejudice, see Synan, *Holiness-Pentecostal Movement*, 80, 109–11, 165–69, 172, 178–79, 182–83, 221; Synan, "Seymour, William Joseph," in *Dictionary of Pentecostal and Charismatic Movements*, ed. Stanley M. Burgess, Gary B. McGee, and Patrick H. Alexander (Grand Rapids: Zondervan, 1988), 778–81; Leonard Lovett, "Black Holiness-Pentecostalism," in *Dictionary of Pentecostal and Charismatic Movements*, 76–84, esp. 83; Burgess, McGee, and Alexander, "The Pentecostal and Charismatic Movements," *Dictionary of Pentecostal and Charismatic Movements*, 3.

26. Stanley M. Burgess, "Evidence of the Spirit: The Medieval and Modern Western Churches," in *Initial Evidence*, 33–34; McGee, "Hermeneutics," 107–8.

27. The focus of our desire should be the Spirit himself and God's purposes in this world, not merely tongues as the evidence of the Spirit. But I suppose that even seeking evidence of the Spirit for the evidence's sake is no more unbiblical than the large number of Christians who never seek an intimate relationship with or empowerment by the Spirit at all (with or without tongues).

28. This is not to say that advocates of the tongues-as-evidence position want people to feel condemned or second-class because they have not spoken in tongues; yet I have sometimes witnessed this phenomenon. I do not here propose a pragmatic test of truth that decides the genuineness of the classical Pentecostal position based on results. Pentecostals could as easily point to their success in worldwide evangelism as a pragmatic proof that their position has God's blessing (which may well be true, at least regarding their emphasis on the Spirit's empowerment). My point is that one can maintain a strong appreciation for the gift, yet articulate it in ways that will commend it to a wider cross-section of the body of Christ, ways that may actually lead to more people sharing the gift even if they do not share all details of classical Pentecostal theology.

Chapter 2: How Important Are Spiritual Gifts Today?

1. For a reasonable and balanced modern cessationist position that does not restrict God's activity as many cessationist positions have, see Daniel B. Wallace, "Who's Afraid of the Holy Spirit?" *Christianity Today*, 12 Sept. 1994, 35–38. For more arguments in favor of cessationism, see Richard B. Gaffin, Jr., *Perspectives on Pentecost* (Phillipsburg, N.J.: Presbyterian and Reformed, 1979); John F. MacArthur, Jr., *Charismatic Chaos* (Grand Rapids: Zondervan, 1992). The cessationist position is difficult for me to identify with, but I have deeply committed Christian friends who hold it, and I do not mean my disagreements to be taken as a lack of respect for them.

2. Charismatics and noncharismatics alike have responded with historical evidence that supernatural gifts continued in some measure in the early centuries of the church; for example, see Ronald A. N. Kydd, *Charismatic Gifts in the Early Church* (Peabody, Mass.: Hendrickson, 1984) and the sources in Siegfried Schatzmann, *A Pauline Theology of Charismata* (Peabody, Mass.: Hendrickson, 1987), 82 n. 40; John Wimber with Kevin Springer, *Power Evangelism* (San Francisco: Harper & Row, 1986), appendix A, 157–74. For a later period, see Stanley M. Burgess, "Evidence of the Spirit: The Ancient and Eastern Churches," 3–19, and "Evidence of the Spirit: The Medieval and Modern Western Churches," 20–40 (esp. 20–26), in *Initial Evidence: Historical and Biblical Perspectives on the Pentecostal Doctrine of Spirit Baptism*, ed. Gary B.

McGee (Peabody, Mass.: Hendrickson, 1991); see also James D. G. Dunn, *Jesus and the Spirit: A Study of the Religious and Charismatic Experience of Jesus and the First Christians as Reflected in the New Testament* (London, SCM, 1975), 192. For a balanced view of charismatic gifts in history, see D. A. Carson, *Showing the Spirit: A Theological Exposition of 1 Corinthians 12–14* (Grand Rapids: Baker, 1987), 165–68. On the second-century church, see especially Gary Shogren, "Christian Prophecy and Canon in the Second Century: A Response to B. B. Warfield," *Journal of the Evangelical Theological Society* (forthcoming). I am grateful to Gary Shogren and his student Kimberlee Johnson for allowing me to examine that manuscript in time for inclusion in the present book.

3. Antisupernaturalism was part of Thomas Paine's Deism (see Mark Noll, *History of Christianity in the United States and Canada* [Grand Rapids: Eerdmans, 1992], 166).

4. See Jack Deere, *Surprised by the Power of the Spirit* (Grand Rapids: Zondervan, 1993), 219–27, for a broader list of arguments. He also supplies responses to many particular objections to which we cannot devote space here.

5. Although the Bible is certainly not against medicine or doctors (1 Tim. 5:23), MacArthur's presentation of Acts 28:9 is tendentious: he thinks this verse represents Luke healing as a physician because the Greek word is different from the term in 28:8 (MacArthur, *Charismatic Chaos*, 219). The difference is undoubtedly due to literary variation, a typical part of Luke's style, however; far from always being nonmiraculous, Luke frequently uses the term for Jesus' healings!

6. Schatzmann, *Pauline Theology of Charismata*, 101 (see also Dunn, *Jesus and the Spirit*, 263, 297). Note the definition of "charismatic" from "charisma" in Schatzmann, 1–7. Such Pauline *charismata* rightly belong to Christ's entire body. Schatzmann, 18, also rightly observes that Paul sometimes applies the term *charisma* to the gift of eternal life (see Rom. 16:23), making *all* Christians "charismatic" in the sense of having received God's gracious gift.

7. For dispensational cessationist arguments on tongues see, for example, C. L. Rogers, "The Gift of Tongues in the Post Apostolic Church (A.D. 100–400)," *Bibliotheca Sacra* 122 (1965): 134–43; Z. C. Hodges, "The Purpose of Tongues," *Bibliotheca Sacra* 120 (1963): 226–33; S. L. Johnson, "The Gift of Tongues and the Book of Acts," *Bibliotheca Sacra* 120 (1963): 309–11; and, on 1 Cor. 12, S. D. Toussaint, "First Corinthians Thirteen and the Tongues Question," *Bibliotheca Sacra* 120 (1963): 311–16. Cessationism is not, however, a mandatory element of modern dispensationalism (see Robert L. Saucy, *The Case for Progressive Dispensationalism* [Grand Rapids: Zondervan, 1993], 186). For another example of newer dispensational approaches see Craig A. Blaising and Darrell L. Bock, *Progressive Dispensationalism* (Wheaton, Ill.: Victor, 1993). We address one of the Reformed approaches below in more detail, via Gaffin; the interested reader will also find more material in Benjamin B. Warfield, *Counterfeit Miracles* (1918; reprint, Carlisle, Pa.: Banner of Truth, 1972) and general articles in *Westminster Theological Journal*.

8. See especially Paul Elbert, "Face to Face: Then or Now?" (paper presented to the seventh annual meeting of the Society for Pentecostal Studies, Springfield, Mo., Dec. 1–3, 1977). Elbert takes into account hundreds of Koine Greek examples to show that this passage refers to the second coming. See also G. D. Fee, *The First Epistle to the Corinthians*, New International Commentary on the New Testament (Grand Rapids: Eerdmans, 1987) and *Gospel and Spirit: Issues in New Testament Hermeneutics*

(Peabody, Mass.: Hendrickson, 1991), 7–8; also G. D. Fee and Douglas Stuart, *How to Read the Bible for All Its Worth* (Grand Rapids: Zondervan, 1982), 60.

9. Gaffin, *Perspectives on Pentecost*, 109. See further Harold Ellis Dollar, "A Cross-Cultural Theology of Healing" (D.Miss. diss., Fuller Theol. Sem. School of World Mission, 1981), 48; Wayne A. Grudem, *The Gift of Prophecy in 1 Corinthians* (Lanham, Md.: University Press of America, 1982), 210–19. For the related view that tongues, prophecy, and knowledge passed away in the church's infancy (faith, hope, and love existing for the present and only love for the future), see R. L. Thomas, "'Tongues . . . Will Cease,'" *Journal of the Evangelical Theological Society* 17 (1974): 81–89. But the passing of the imperfect and the arriving of maturity corresponds in 1 Cor. 13:12 to seeing Christ face to face, and Paul's "now abides" refers to the time of Christ's return, since "greatest" in 13:13 is not temporal. D. A. Carson has shown that the Greek middle form of "cease" (1 Cor. 13:8) does not here mean "cease of themselves" and that New Testament usage does not support such a distinction (*Exegetical Fallacies*, 2d ed. [Grand Rapids: Baker, 1996], 76–77; see also *Showing the Spirit*, 66–67).

Later Jewish teachers understood Jer. 31:31–34 as promising the fullness of knowledge in the age to come (W. D. Davies, *Paul and Rabbinic Judaism*, 4th ed. [Philadelphia: Fortress, 1980], 224; compare the Babylonian Talmud, *Shabbat* 63b, in Davies, *Torah in the Messianic Age and/or the Age to Come,* Journal of Biblical Literature Monograph Series 7 [Philadelphia: Society of Biblical Literature, 1952], 82). The idea that one can have perfect knowledge in *this* age Irenaeus attributes to Gnosticism (*Against Heresies* 2.28).

10. Mirrors were not necessarily poor reflectors (Wisdom of Solomon 7:26; Odes of Solomon 13.1–4), but Greek writers sometimes apply the term metaphorically to understanding the divine (see F. G. Downing, "Reflecting the First Century: 1 Corinthians 13:12," *Expository Times* 95 [1984]: 176–77; D. H. Gill, "Through a Glass, Darkly: A Note on 1 Corinthians 13,12," *Catholic Biblical Quarterly* 25 [1963]: 427–29; contrast, less likely, R. Seaford, "1 Corinthians XIII.12," *Journal of Theological Studies* 35 [1984]: 117–20). For the Moses allusion here see David Hill, *New Testament Prophecy* (Atlanta: John Knox, 1979), 137; F. F. Bruce, *1 and 2 Corinthians*, New Century Bible 38 (Greenwood, S.C.: Attic Press, 1971), 128; James Moffatt, *The First Epistle of Paul to the Corinthians,* Moffatt New Testament Commentary (London: Hodder & Stoughton, 1938), 201; M. Fishbane, "Through the Looking Glass: Reflections on Ezek 43:3, Num 12:8 and 1 Cor 13," *Hebrew Annual Review* 10 (1986): 63–75.

11. Grand Rapids: Zondervan, 1993.

12. Deere, *Surprised*, 134–43.

13. Fee, *Gospel and Spirit*, 77.

14. Whatever "apostles" specifically means, of course, it does not require us to believe that anyone can add to Scripture today; the canon is by definition closed, a measuring-stick of all other revelation. Some who may fit the biblical definition of apostle today probably believe apostles have ceased! True apostles must be servants, never people who "pull rank" (compare Acts 15:22; 1 Cor. 4:9–16; 2 Cor. 11:5–15; Col. 1:24–25). Being an apostle need presuppose having "seen" Jesus (1 Cor. 9:1) no more than being "free" in the same passage does.

15. Sometimes biblical writers use "first, second, third" merely to summarize chronologically without ranking (Gen. 32:19; Matt. 22:25–26). But in 1 Cor. 12:28 Paul ennumerates specific items where chronology is irrelevant and numbering was

unnecessary. In contrast to many scholars, I believe that the listing of at least the first three offices, with apostles at the top, does suggest rank.

16. Compare Michael Green, *I Believe in the Holy Spirit*, 2d rev. ed. (Grand Rapids: Eerdmans, 1989), 252–53; Carson, *Showing the Spirit*, 41–42. For the use of the imperative in 1 Cor. 12:31 and 14:1, 39, see also Carson, *Showing the Spirit*, 57–58.

17. Carson, *Showing the Spirit*, 40.

18. On this point I differ from Wayne Grudem, although I am in sympathy with his basic direction on prophecy and greatly appreciate his important work on the subject; see my *Paul, Women, and Wives* (Peabody, Mass.: Hendrickson, 1992), 245. Grudem's primary concern seems to be to keep canonical revelation on a higher level than any current prophecies, which must be tested by what has already been proved and now constitutes Scripture. I am in full agreement with this concern and with the absolute priority of canonical revelation; see below under the gift of "discernment of spirits."

19. Acts 19:6 exhibits a special construction, distinguishing "speaking in tongues" from "prophesying"; the Greek wording of Acts 10:46 technically allows tongues and praise to be identified.

20. See the various responses, pro and con, to William Graham McDonald's "Biblical Glossolalia—Thesis 7," *Paraclete* (Spring 1994) and *Paraclete* (Winter 1995), including articles by David Bundrick and Benny Aker. Bundrick cites others within the Assemblies of God who hold that the primary function of public tongues is prayer (Anthony Palma and Gordon Fee) and notes that it does not violate the denomination's doctrinal parameters (Bundrick himself finds some implicit scriptural support for the position).

21. Paul's view of self-edification in 1 Cor. 14:4 cannot be negative, since he encourages private uninterpreted tongues in 14:5 (Carson, *Showing the Spirit*, 102 n. 89).

22. Carson, *Showing the Spirit*, 84–86.

23. Jack Deere, in fact, provides a complete listing of miracles in various periods (*Surprised*, appendix C, 253–66).

Chapter 3: How Can We Recognize the Spirit?

1. To better grasp how ancient readers would have understood these texts portraying the kindness of God, see for example Craig Keener, *The IVP Bible Background Commentary: New Testament* (Downers Grove, Ill.: InterVarsity, 1993), 95, 167, 232.

2. See Philo *On Sobriety* 55; Isocrates *To Demonicus* (oration 1) 24–25; Josephus *Against Apion* 2.207.

3. On Abraham as God's friend, see 2 Chron. 20:7; Isa. 41:8; see also Amos 3:7; Philo *On Abraham* 273.

4. See Martial *Epigrams* 2.43.1–16; Diogenes Laertius *Lives of Eminent Philosophers* 6.2.37, 72; 7.1.125.

5. Downers Grove, Ill.: InterVarsity, 1993.

6. That the particular forms of dancing are often culturally expressed may be illustrated by some traditional African American churches, where specific forms of dance (like the "shout," with roots in African emotional worship) become a vehicle for expressing exuberance about God's presence, or by many Messianic Jewish congregations, where the horah and other dances are incorporated into the often charismatic worship.

7. In keeping with traditional Jewish usage, "in the Spirit" probably suggests the Spirit's inspiration, although this could include worship in one's own language (1 Chron. 25:1–7) as well as in tongues.

8. The latter example is the more remarkable considering Saul's inspiration from an "evil spirit" in 1 Sam. 18:10. Although the nature of this spirit is debated and some of my knowledgeable colleagues in Old Testament studies doubt that 1 Sam. 18:10 refers to a demon, I am inclined to think that it probably does.

9. J. Lee Grady, *What Happened to the Fire? Rekindling the Blaze of Charismatic Renewal* (Grand Rapids: Chosen Books, 1994).

10. Examples of "self-promoting" revelations could likewise be multiplied. In 1965, Homer Tomlinson, son of a former overseer of a Pentecostal denomination, announced that he was king of the world. Like other "end-time prophets" before him such as John Alexander Dowie or William Branham, however, his revelation failed to commend itself to most of his subjects. He died in 1969 (Vinson Synan, *The Holiness-Pentecostal Movement in the United States* [Grand Rapids: Eerdmans, 1971], 196–97).

11. John F. MacArthur, Jr., *Charismatic Chaos* (Grand Rapids: Zondervan, 1992), throughout.

12. Ibid., 80–81.

13. Ibid., 75, for example.

Appendix: What Can Bible Stories Teach Us?

1. Gordon Fee's *God's Empowering Presence: The Holy Spirit in the Letters of Paul* (Peabody, Mass.: Hendrickson, 1994) is the most extensive in this regard; D. A. Carson's *Showing the Spirit: A Theological Exposition of 1 Corinthians 12–14* (Grand Rapids: Baker, 1987) is also excellent and is probably the best work devoted specifically to spiritual gifts.

Selected Bibliography

Burgess, Stanley M., Gary B. McGee, and Patrick H. Alexander, eds. *Dictionary of Pentecostal and Charismatic Movements*. Grand Rapids: Zondervan, 1988. The most complete set of articles providing perspectives on the Pentecostal and charismatic movements.

Carson, D. A. *Showing the Spirit: A Theological Exposition of 1 Corinthians 12–14*. Grand Rapids: Baker, 1987. Currently the best evangelical treatment of the gifts of the Spirit, containing an enormous amount of relevant documentation in a relatively brief book. Carson is fair to all the evidence and will appeal especially to those seeking a mediating position between Pentecostalism and cessationism.

Deere, Jack. *Surprised by the Power of the Spirit*. Grand Rapids: Zondervan, 1993. A former Dallas Theological Seminary professor and cessationist mounts an impressive case against the cessationist position both from the Bible and from eyewitness accounts of miracles God is doing today. He claims that cessationists argue from a lack of experience of what God is doing today.

Dunn, James D. G. *Baptism in the Holy Spirit: A Re-examination of the New Testament Teaching on the Gift of the Spirit in Relation to Pentecostalism Today*. Philadelphia: Westminster; London: SCM, 1970. One of the most thorough scholarly treatments of Spirit baptism in the New Testament, now regarded as a classic. Without disputing the continuing validity of the gifts today, Dunn insists that the New Testament does not teach a "second baptism."

Fee, Gordon D. *God's Empowering Presence: The Holy Spirit in the Letters of Paul*. Peabody, Mass.: Hendrickson, 1994. The most thorough treatment available on the Spirit in Paul's letters, including both commentary and synthesis. A Pentecostal scholar, Fee finds no evidence for a "second baptism" in Paul, but rather (like Dunn) he refers Pauline language of Spirit reception to conversion.

———. *Gospel and Spirit: Issues in New Testament Hermeneutics.* Peabody, Mass.: Hendrickson, 1991. Fee treats many of the interpretive issues for which no space could be provided in our book. Although I would restrict the value of historical precedent less than he does, he provides an insightful evangelical-Pentecostal hermeneutic.

Gaffin, Richard B., Jr. *Perspectives on Pentecost: Studies in New Testament Teaching on the Gifts of the Holy Spirit.* Phillipsburg, N.J.: Presbyterian and Reformed, 1979. Gaffin argues that apostleship, prophecy, and tongues (as a form of prophecy) were foundational gifts and have therefore ceased. Those who do not agree with this reasoning (including myself) will nevertheless find many points of sound and helpful exegesis elsewhere in the book.

Green, Michael. *I Believe in the Holy Spirit.* 2d rev. ed. Grand Rapids: Eerdmans, 1989. Written on a popular level but informed by sound scholarship, this work argues for baptism in the Holy Spirit as initiation rather than a second experience. At the same time, Green contends that the Pentecostal/charismatic experience is valid (just misnamed) and that all gifts are for today (though tongues is not a special badge).

Hollenweger, Walter J. *The Pentecostals.* Translated by R. A. Wilson. London: SCM Press, 1972; reprint, Peabody, Mass.: Hendrickson, 1988. Original German edition, *Enthusiastisches Christentum: Die Pfingstbewegung in Geschichte und Gegenwart.* Zurich: Zwingli, 1969. This represents the most comprehensive survey of Pentecostalism in its various forms and its history to date. The book emphasizes the experiential unity but doctrinal diversity of the movement.

Keener, Craig S. *The Spirit in the Gospels and Acts.* Peabody, Mass.: Hendrickson, 1995. This work traces examples of the two primary themes in early Jewish pneumatology (purification and prophetic enablement) through early Christian narratives, providing more-detailed and better-documented arguments for some of the claims in *3 Crucial Questions about the Holy Spirit.*

Lederle, Henry I. *Treasures Old and New: Interpretations of "Spirit-Baptism" in the Charismatic Renewal Movement.* Peabody, Mass.: Hendrickson,

1988. A carefully arranged survey of the many diverse views on Spirit baptism among charismatics (including sacramental views among charismatic Catholics, Spirit baptism at conversion, etc.) by a charismatic in the Reformed tradition.

MacArthur, John F., Jr. *Charismatic Chaos*. Grand Rapids: Zondervan, 1992. A popular and sensitive argument for the cessationist view of supernatural spiritual gifts.

McGee, Gary B., editor. *Initial Evidence: Historical and Biblical Perspectives on the Pentecostal Doctrine of Spirit Baptism*. Peabody, Mass.: Hendrickson, 1991. Essays examine various views throughout history on evidences of the Spirit's work, including diverse interpretations in twentieth-century Pentecostal history. Theological treatments include both charismatic and noncharismatic views.

Mills, Watson E. *The Holy Spirit: A Bibliography*. Peabody, Mass.: Hendrickson, 1988. This volume contains the most complete listing of sources up to 1988 (2,098 entries), including unpublished dissertations, privately published materials, foreign language works, scholarly articles, and historical as well as exegetical works. Mills covers the whole range of views and subjects.

Stronstad, Roger. *The Charismatic Theology of Saint Luke*. Foreword by Clark Pinnock. Peabody, Mass.: Hendrickson, 1984. A brief and simple, yet thorough and nuanced, argument for the Pentecostal position on Acts, including a response to Dunn.

Synan, Vinson. *The Holiness-Pentecostal Movement in the United States*. Grand Rapids: Eerdmans, 1971. This work traces the history of the early Pentecostal movement, including its understanding of baptism in the Holy Spirit.

Williams, J. Rodman. *Renewal Theology*. 3 vols. Grand Rapids: Academie Books, Zondervan, 1990. See especially volume 2, *Salvation, the Holy Spirit, and Christian Living,* addressing the Holy Spirit in a charismatic theology by a charismatic in the Reformed tradition who teaches at Regent University, Virginia.

Wimber, John, with Kevin Springer. *Power Evangelism*. San Francisco: Harper & Row, 1986. A call to the church to reappropriate the biblical use of signs and wonders in evangelism.

Scripture Index

Genesis
1:2 108
2:7 35
6:3 154
18:17 145
18:27 86
18:30 86
18:32 86
32:19 197 n. 15
41:38 143

Exodus
2:23 48
2:24 48
4:22 48
4:24–26 138
7:8–13 192 n. 8
12:12 192 n. 8
13:21 48
15:20–21 135
19:6 42
20:5–6 139
28:3 109
31:3 109
32:35 138
33:3 139
33:11 97, 145
33:17 139
33:18 139
33:19–23 139
34:5–7 139
34:6–7 139

34:8–9 140
34:10 140
35:31 109

Leviticus
23:10 30

Numbers
11:17 109
11:25–26 109
11:25–29 24, 108
11:29 23–24
12:1 42
24:2 108
27:18 109, 143
33:53–54 48

Deuteronomy
7:9–10 139
30:11–14 154
34:9 109
34:10 145

Judges
3:10 109
6:13 80
6:34 60, 109
8:35 160
11:29 109
13:25 60, 109
14:6 109
14:19 60, 109
15:14 109

1 Samuel
9:6–9 105
9:6–10 117
9:6–20 146
9:20 105
10:5 117, 135
10:5–6 121
10:6 50, 60, 108, 109
10:10 50, 108, 109
11:6 109
16:13–14 109
18:10 199 n. 8
19:20 60, 108, 119, 121, 147
19:20–23 23
19:20–24 165
19:21–24 129
19:23 108

2 Samuel
23:2 24, 108
23:2–3 117

1 Kings
1:1 115
13:1–6 116
13:11 42
14:1–3 116
17:4 42
17:13–14 117
17:13–16 39
17:17–24 39
17–19 42

18:12 108–9
18:13 44, 119
18:20–40 192 n. 8
18:33–35 43
18:36 43, 113, 116
18:40 44
19:1–2 44
19:3–5 44
19:19–21 39, 43
21:17–18 113
22:24 108

2 Kings
1:8 26
1:10 116
2:3–8 147
2:9 40, 108
2:14 129
2:15 40, 108, 119
3:15 117, 135
4:1 42–43
4:3–4 117
4:27 113
4:32–37 39
4:38 119
4:42–44 39
5:9 43
5:26 113
5:26–27 42
6:12 113
13:14 115
13:20–21 115

1 Chronicles
6:31–32 135
12:18 108
15:16 135
15:28–29 135
16:4–6 135
23:27 135
23:30 135
25:1–7 135, 162, 199
  n. 7
25:1–8 117

2 Chronicles
8:14 135
15:1 108
15:1–7 24

18:23 24, 108
20:7 198 n. 3
20:14 108
20:20–22 135
20:20–24 135
24:16 160
24:20 108
29:25 135
29:30 135
31:2 135

Ezra
3:10–11 135

Nehemiah
9:20 144
9:25 160
9:30 108
9:35 160
12:24 135
12:27 135
12:36 135
12:43 135
12:45–46 135

Job
12:5 114
27:3 35
33:4 108
42:7–8 114
42:10 115

Psalms
5:11 158
9:14 158
12:1 117
12:5 117
13:5 158
23:3 149
25:4–5 149
25:8–10 149
30:11 158
32:11 158
35:27 158
37:3–7 116
42:4 158
43:4 158
46:1 117
46:10 117, 158

48:2 158
48:11 158
51:11 109
52:3 160
63:7 158
67:4 158
71:23 158
78:17–31 138
91:3 117
91:14–16 117
104:30 108
105:43 158
110:1 37, 89
119:162 158
132:9 158
132:16 158
139:7 108
143:10 144
149:2 158
149:3 158
150:4 158

Proverbs
1:7 151
1:23 144
15:1 161

Ecclesiastes
4:8 160
5:11 160
6:6 160
9:18 160

Isaiah
1:15–17 118
2:2 89
8:3 43
11:2 109
26:9–10 116
31:3 154
32:15 35
34:16 108
35:5–6 88
40:7 108
40:13 133
41:8 198 n. 3
42:1 24, 108
43:10 108
44:1–5 108

44:3 24, 36, 89
48:3–5 116
48:16 108, 133
57:19 89
58:1–14 118
59:21 24, 108
61:1 108
63:10–11 133
63:10–14 148
66:15–16 36

Jeremiah
16:2–4 43
22:13–17 118
22:16 147
23:16–32 173
23:21–22 120
25:15 117
27:2 117
28:8–9 173
28:12–17 117
31:31–34 154, 197
  n. 9
31:33 155
31:33–34 48
31:34 97
36:4–8 117

Lamentations
3:37 116
3:37–38 43

Ezekiel
1:28 108
2:1–2 108
2:2 108
3:12 23, 108
3:14 108
3:24 108
8:3 108
11:1 108
11:5 108
11:24 108
13:3 119
18:31 24
24:18 43
34:2–4 106
36:24–28 36
36:25–27 32

36:26–27 24, 48, 154
36:27 142, 155
37 36
37:1 108
37:5–14 35
37:14 24, 36
39:29 24, 36
43:5 108
47:1–6 33

Daniel
4:8–9 143
4:18 143
5:11 143
5:14 143

Hosea
1:2 117
2:8–10 138
11:1–7 138

Joel
2:27–3:1 36
2:28 37
2:28–29 24, 37, 137
2:32 89
3:1 37

Amos
3:7 198 n. 3
3:7–8 116
5:7–24 118

Micah
3:8 24, 108
4:1 89

Habakkuk
3:19 117, 135

Zephaniah
1:18 36
3:8 36

Zechariah
3:6–9 42
4:2 42
4:2–3 42
4:6 109
4:6–14 42
4:11 42

7:5–10 129
7:12 108
14:8 33

Malachi
4:5–6 26

Matthew
3:2 27, 88
3:4 26
3:7 26
3:7–8 27
3:9 26
3:10 27
3:11 25
3:12 27
4:17 88
6:9–10 110
6:11 110
6:25–34 110
6:33 110
7:7–11 110
7:21–23 129, 165
8 86
8:1–4 86
8:2 86
8:3 86
8:17 87
8:18–22 86
9 86
9:9–17 86
9:18–19 86
9:20–21 86
9:22 87
9:35 88
9:35–36 114
9:35–38 86
9:36 87, 88
9:37 87
9:37–38 87
9:38 87
10 87
10:5–6 87, 88
10:7 88
10:8 88
10:17–39 88
10:20 25
10:23 88

10:40–42 88
11:2–3 28
11:4–6 88
11:29 161
12:18 192 n. 4
12:19–20 161
12:24 192 n. 4
12:28 192 n. 4
12:31–32 192 n. 4
17:16–17 115
17:19–20 115
18:24–27 138
21:5 161
22:25–26 197 n. 15
22:43 25
28:18–19 88
28:19 87–88, 133

Mark

1:7–13 29
1:8 29
1:10 29
1:12 29
1:41 86, 114
2:8 113
3:22–29 29
4:30–32 28
4:40 115
8:31–38 188
9:18–19 115
9:28–29 115
10:33–45 188
11:15–16 161
11:23 113
12:6 138
12:29–31 157
12:36 29
12:38–40 161
13:9–13 188
13:11 29
14:21–51 188
14:31–51 188

Luke

1:15 50
1:15–17 35
1:17 25, 39, 40
1:41–42 35, 50

1:67 35, 50
2:1 37
2:20 91
2:26 35
2:27 25
3:9 36
3:16 35
3:16–17 36
4:18 25
4:18–19 35
4:24–27 39
7:11–17 39
9:10–17 39
9:30 39
9:61–62 39, 43
11:1–13 127
12:12 35
12:47–48 134
15:12 138
16:9–15 169
24:47–49 40
24:49 36

John

1:1–13 139
1:14 139, 140
1:16 139
1:17 140
1:18 140
1:31–33 32
1:45–46 137
1:47–51 140
1:49 137
2:6 32
2:11 140
2:16 143
3:3 31
3:4 31
3:5–8 25
3:6 32
3:8 35
3:16 31, 141
3:18–19 144
3:36 31
4 32–33
4:13–14 34
4:14 33, 34
4:17 33

4:23–24 162
4:24 135, 136
4:28–42 33
5:5–9 33
5:39 138
5:45–47 138
6:53–71 34
7:18 145
7:37–38 34
7:37–39 32, 33
7:39 34, 145
8:28 34
8:31 34
8:46 144
8:59 34
9 33
9:28–29 138
9:39–10:10 138
10:3 138
10:4–5 137
10:10 173
10:14 137
10:41 40
12:23–24 140
12:23–25 34
12:32–33 34, 140, 173
13:31–38 142
13:34–35 147, 157,
  180, 182
14:1–3 142
14:2 142, 143
14:2–3 143
14:3 142
14:5 142
14:6 143, 148
14:9 138
14:16–17 133, 142
14:16–20 142
14:16–23 142
14:17 134
14:18 142
14:19 142
14:23 142, 143
14:23–24 142
14:26 34, 144, 146
15 143
15:1–11 142

15:1–17 156
15:4–7 143
15:9–10 143
15:9–14 147
15:12 157
15:15 145
15:17 147
15:22 144
15:26 146
15:26–27 144
15:26–16:11 34–35
16 144
16:7 144, 145
16:8–11 144
16:12–15 34, 144, 145
16:13 145, 146, 148
16:13–15 133
16:14 134, 146
16:14–15 145, 146
16:16 142, 145
16:20–22 142
16:28 143
17:1–5 34
17:4 145
18:23 161
19:34 34
20:14–15 138
20:16 138
20:19–23 35
20:20–22 145
20:21 35
20:22 35, 142
21:25 186

Acts

1:1 40
1:2 35
1:4–5 36, 50, 59, 89
1:4–8 36
1:5 193 n. 10
1:6–7 36
1:8 25, 35, 36, 40, 66,
  69, 73, 168
1:17 58
2 35–38, 54, 66–67,
  90
2:1–4 36, 60, 193
  n. 10

2:4 21, 35, 50, 60, 90,
  118, 168
2:5–13 37
2:5–41 91
2:9–11 168
2:11 121
2:12 66
2:12–13 37
2:13 66
2:14 60
2:14–21 37
2:15 67
2:15–16 37
2:16–18 37, 67, 105,
  118
2:16–21 35
2:17 35, 37, 89
2:17–18 37, 168
2:18 38
2:19–21 67
2:21 38, 89, 90
2:22–41 38
2:25 89
2:33 50, 91
2:33–35 89
2:34–35 37
2:34–36 89
2:38 21, 38, 51, 56, 90
2:38–39 50, 89
2:39 38, 50, 89, 90
2:41 56
2:41–42 169
2:42 169, 176
2:42–44 159
2:42–47 38
2:43 55, 91, 169
2:44 169
2:44–45 168–70, 170
2:45 169
2:46–47 169
3:6–7 55
3:11–4:4 91
3:12–13 43
4:4 55
4:7 30
4:8 21, 35, 50, 60, 68
4:20 91

4:29–30 127
4:29–31 91, 93
4:30 55
4:31 21, 35, 50, 60,
  68, 73
4:32 169
4:34–37 170
4:35 169
5:3–5 133
5:4 169
5:10–11 91
5:12 91
5:12–16 55, 91
5:15–16 114
5:16 116
5:16–18 30
5:32 35
6 37
6:1–6 169
6:3 91
6:3–7 55
6:5 91
6:7 36, 92
6:8 55, 91
6:8–10 91
6:10 25, 35
7:51 35
7:55 35
8 54, 56, 57, 58–59,
  67, 69
8:4 37, 91, 92
8:4–5 55
8:5 55
8:6–7 91
8:6–8 55
8:7 114
8:12 55
8:13 91
8:14 56, 92
8:14–17 59, 110
8:15 56
8:15–16 21, 50
8:18–24 58
8:25 37
8:29 25, 35, 147, 149
8:39–40 91
9 54, 67

9:5 52
9:5–6 52
9:8 52
9:10 53
9:17 21, 50, 52, 59, 60
9:18 56
9:31 36
9:34–35 91
9:36 53
9:40–42 91
10 51, 52, 54
10:19 25, 35, 147, 149
10:38 35, 192 n. 4
10:44 50, 59, 92
10:44–47 90, 193
  n. 10
10:45 50, 55
10:45–46 35, 68
10:46 121, 198 n. 19
10:46–47 67
10:47 50, 56, 90
11:1 56
11:12 25, 147, 149
11:14 51
11:14–15 59
11:15–16 193 n. 10
11:15–17 50
11:17 55
11:17–18 37
11:18 56
11:27 105
11:28 25, 35, 118
11:28–30 18
12:24 36
13:1 103, 105
13:2 35
13:4 35
13:9 21, 35, 60
13:9–10 50
13:9–12 91
13:24 56
13:44 92
13:48 55
13:52 50, 55, 60
13–28 104
14:1–2 55
14:3 55, 91, 92, 126,

127
14:3–6 30
14:4 104
14:9 91, 113
14:15 56
15:4 104
15:7 55
15:7–11 51
15:9 55
15:12 91
15:22 197 n. 14
15:28 35
16:1 53, 55
16:5 36
16:6–9 35
16:7 25
16:18 116
16:25–34 91
16:31–34 55
16:32 92
16:33 56
16:34 58
17:2–3 91
17:11 56
17:12 55
17:13 92
17:30 56
17:34 55
18:8 55, 56, 58
18:28 91
19 53, 54
19:2 50, 56
19:4–6 21, 59
19:5 56, 58
19:5–6 59
19:6 50, 53, 67, 68,
  90, 198 n. 19
19:8–10 91
19:11–12 55
19:11–20 91
19:18 55
19:18–19 57–58
19:20 36, 92
20:17 106
20:21 56
20:23 35, 117
20:25 55

20:28 106
21:4 25, 35, 117
21:10 105, 118
21:11 35, 117, 118
22:10 52
22:16 52, 58, 192 n. 6
26:15–16 52
26:18 56
27:25 58
28:5–6 91
28:8 196 n. 5
28:8–9 114
28:8–10 91
28:9 196 n. 5
28:31 36, 55

Romans
1–3 94
1:2 49
1:4 47
2:4 160
2:12–16 134
3:12 160
4:1–5:11 94
4:5 50
4:17 116
5:1 159
5:2 142
5:5 21, 47, 141, 152
5:6–8 141
5:12–21 94
6:1–11 48
6:3–4 49
6:4–5 156
6:11 156
6:11–14 49
6:18 48
6:20 48
6:22 48
7:7–25 94
7:14 48
7:17–18 48
8 30, 48, 49, 149
8:2 48
8:2–10 154
8:5–6 151
8:6 158
8:9 47, 48, 134

8:9–11 49
8:11 192 n. 4
8:13 49, 156
8:14 48
8:14–16 48, 49
8:15 48
8:15–17 149
8:16 141, 149,
150–51, 152
8:16–18 30
8:17 48
8:18 149
8:22–23 30, 149
8:23 30, 48, 49
8:26 30, 149
8:26–27 49, 133
8:26–30 30
8:28–30 149
9 94
9–11 95
9:22 160
11 94
11:22 160
12 93, 103, 107
12:1 95, 118
12:2 95, 151
12:3 95, 113
12:4–8 77, 94, 95,
110, 179
12:4–16 94
12:6 107, 113
12:7 107
12:8 118
12:18 159
13:8–10 94, 157
14 94
14:17 154
14:19 159
15:7–12 94
15:14 160
15:15–32 94
15:19 25
15:30 154
16:7 104
16:17 178

1 Corinthians
1–4 95, 112

1:5 96, 164
1:5–7 112
1:7 164
1:10 164
1:17 96
1:18 130
1:18–2:16 112
2:4 25
2:4–5 130
2:6–8 130
2:10–14 25
2:10–16 47
2:12 47
2:12–16 30
3:1–3 48
3:10 104
3:16 143
4:9–16 197 n. 14
4:21 161
5–7 95
5:2 165
6:11 25, 48
6:19 144
7:9 161
7:15 159
7:21 164
7:40 25
8–11 96
8:1 165
8:1–3 112
9 95
9:1 197 n. 14
9:25 161
10:11 190
11:17–34 70
12 62, 93, 100, 103,
164
12–14 98–101, 116,
122, 164–68
12:1–3 165
12:3 25
12:4–11 165
12:4–30 40
12:7 77, 96, 99, 110
12:7–13 84
12:8 96, 111
12:8–10 110–25

12:8–11 107
12:10 111
12:11 109
12:12–26 165, 168
12:12–27 99
12:13 34
12:14–26 179
12:15–26 96
12:27–30 165
12:28 84, 105, 110,
116, 197 n. 15
12:28–30 109
12:28–31 84
12:29 118
12:29–30 110
12:30 71, 72
12:31 99, 109, 165,
166, 198 n. 16
13 96–98, 109, 164,
165, 180
13:1 111
13:1–2 110
13:1–3 97, 165
13:2 113, 115
13:4 160
13:4–8 165
13:8 97, 112, 197 n. 9
13:8–9 110
13:8–10 81
13:8–12 99
13:8–13 85, 97, 165
13:9 97, 112, 119
13:10 102
13:12 97, 137, 197
n. 9
13:13 157, 161, 197
n. 9
14 62, 165, 166
14:1 99, 106, 109,
165, 166, 198 n. 16
14:1–5 96
14:2–5 96, 111
14:3 118, 122
14:4 122, 166, 198
n. 21
14:5 71–72, 96, 99,
118, 121, 122, 198

n. 21
14:13–16 122
14:13–17 96
14:13–19 121
14:14–15 100
14:14–16 122
14:14–17 121
14:14–19 166
14:15 136
14:18 67, 99, 100,
  108, 177
14:18–19 96, 121, 122
14:19 96
14:20 129
14:23–25 122
14:24–25 113, 116
14:26 18, 110, 113,
  162
14:27–28 96
14:28 96, 121
14:29 119, 120, 147,
  176
14:29–31 116
14:29–32 118
14:29–33 100
14:30 18, 113
14:31 105, 118
14:32 119
14:32–33 100
14:37–38 103
14:39 99, 166, 198
  n. 16
14:39–40 119
14:40 99
15:5–7 104

2 Corinthians

1:22 31
3:2–18 140
3:3–8 25
3:7–18 97
5:5 31
6:1–6 160
6:6 160
8–9 170
8:23 104
10:1 161
11:5–15 197 n. 14

11:18–12:10 130
12:1 108
12:1–10 108
13:3–4 130
13:9 130
13:13 133
13:14 159

Galatians

1:12 18
1:16 18
2:2 18
2:11–14 119
2:20 154, 156
3:2 21, 47
3:2–5 21, 154, 161
3:3 47
3:5 49
4:6 152
4:13–14 115, 126
4:29 25, 156
5:5 154, 161
5:5–6 157
5:6 157
5:13 155
5:13–14 155
5:13–15 157
5:13–6:10 149, 154
5:14 157
5:15 155
5:16 155, 156
5:16–23 21, 49
5:16–25 154–62
5:17 155
5:17–18 25
5:18 149, 155, 157
5:19–21 155
5:22 157
5:22–23 157
5:22–6:2 85
5:23 157
5:24 156
5:24–25 154, 156
5:25 156
5:25–6:10 157
5:26–6:2 157
6:1 157, 161
6:2 157

6:7–8 154
6:8 25
6:14 156
6:15 156

Ephesians

1:13 47, 105
1:13–14 31, 47
1:17 25
1:19–20 47
2 103
2:7 160
2:14–15 159
2:17 89
2:18 142, 145
2:20 81, 101, 102, 105
2:22 143
3:5 25, 101, 105
3:8–9 102
3:8–13 101
3:16 145
3:16–19 141, 152
3:17–19 144
4 93, 103–7
4:2 160, 161
4:3 159, 168
4:3–5 103
4:3–13 85
4:4–12 159
4:7 103
4:8 103
4:11 101, 103, 110, 118
4:11–13 107
4:12 103
4:12–13 104, 106
4:13 159
4:23 151
4:24 156
4:25–32 154
4:25–5:2 159
4:30 46–47
4:32 160
5:9 157, 160
5:18 21, 47, 49, 162
5:18–20 73, 136
5:18–21 162–64
5:19–20 162
5:21 162

5:25 163
6:4 164
6:9 164
6:15 105, 159
6:17 25, 105
6:18 121, 136, 162

Philippians

1:9 156
1:10–11 156
1:11 157
1:19 49
1:27–2:4 159
2:1 154, 159
2:5–11 159
2:16–18 159
2:19–24 159
2:25–30 159
2:27 115, 126
3:3 135, 136
3:9–10 142
3:10 153
4:2–3 159
4:2–9 159
4:4–7 158
4:7–8 151

Colossians

1:4–5 157
1:6 157
1:8 154
1:10 156, 157, 160
1:11 156, 159
1:12 156
1:24–25 197 n. 14
1:28 44, 184
2:6–23 21
3:2 151
3:3 49
3:5 49
3:12 160, 161
3:12–13 160
3:12–14 160
3:15 159

1 Thessalonians

1:3 157
2:13 154
4:8 154

5:13 159
5:14 160
5:16–18 158
5:19 25, 119
5:20 100
5:20–22 119, 176

2 Thessalonians

1:11 160
2:2 25
3:16 159

1 Timothy

1:18 126
2:7 103
3:1 106
3:2 84
3:2–7 106
4:1 25
4:14 104, 126
5:23 115, 196 n. 5

2 Timothy

1:6 126
1:11 103
2:14 19
2:24 84, 104
2:25 161
3:16 54, 187
4:5 104
4:20 115, 126

Titus

1:5–7 106
1:9 84
3:4 160

Hebrews

2:1–3 125
2:3–4 125
2:4 125
4:16 141
6:4–5 30
9:14 192 n. 4
11:8–19 41
11:23–29 41
11:35–38 41

James

1:21 161

2:14 50
3:1 134
3:13 161
3:14–18 158
3:17 157
4:1–4 116
5:1–6 118
5:10–11 159
5:13 158
5:14–15 114
5:14–16 41, 115
5:14–18 115
5:17 43
5:17–18 41, 115

1 Peter

1:2 154
1:10–11 23
1:11 25, 143
1:22 154, 159
2:5 135, 143
2:9 135
3:15 161
3:18 192 n. 4
4:10 179
4:10–11 93, 110–11
4:14 143
5:1–4 106
5:5 179

2 Peter

1:4–11 162
1:21 23

1 John

2:1 144
2:3–6 182
2:20 144
2:23 134
2:27 144
3:6 154
3:9 154
3:21–24 42
3:24 141
4:1–6 25, 119
4:2 146
4:2–6 144
4:7–8 147, 153
4:13 137, 141

5:6–8 141
5:14 113
5:14–15 42
5:18 154

Jude
19 25, 178
20 121, 122, 136, 162

Revelation
1:6 42, 135
1:10 25

1:20 42
2:1 118
2:7 25
3:1 118
3:6 25
4:2 25
5:9–10 37
5:10 42
7:9 37
11:3–6 42
11:4 42

11:6 42
11:11 192 n. 4
13:7 37
13:16 37
14:13 25
17:3 25
19:10 25, 105, 118
21:10 25
22:1 34
22:6 119
22:17 25, 34